The Gospel & Sexual Orientation

A Testimony of the
Reformed Presbyterian Church of North America

Edited by Michael LeFebvre

7408 Penn Avenue,
Pittsburgh, Pa., 15208

Printed in the United States of America

ISBN: 978-1-884527-37-1 (paperback)
ISBN: 978-1-884527-52-4 (ePub)
ISBN: 978-1-884527-53-1 (Kindle)

Library of Congress Control Number: 2012933828

Arno Pro was used for the body text and headers.

Contents

Foreword

The New Testament church was filled with controversies. In fact, many of the New Testament epistles were written to address moral and doctrinal conflicts raging in first century congregations. We should not be surprised, therefore, if controversies emerge in the church today. Inevitably, when the church is doing what she is supposed to be doing—namely, living out the Gospel in engagement with the world—vigorous questions will emerge about how the two relate. But how should the church handle such controversies?

The fifteenth chapter of Acts points the way. When a congregation in first-century Antioch became embroiled in one of the raging debates of that time, the church leadership did not ignore the issue. Instead, the question was taken seriously and, when local instruction was unable to resolve it, delegates from Antioch were sent to Jerusalem to consult with the Apostles and with elders from the wider church. According to that chapter, the assembly considered relevant pastoral concerns and the witness of Scripture on the subject; then a written, unified testimony was prepared. A document was published for instruction and pastoral guidance in the wider church.

Throughout history, churches have continued this practice of engaging moral and doctrinal controversies in ecclesiastical assemblies (councils, presbyteries, general assemblies, etc.), writing up conclusions in the form of creeds, confessions, circular letters, or other documents of unified, public testimony. This book, *The Gospel and Sexual Orientation*, participates (in a small way) in that heritage of the church.

Without a doubt, homosexuality is one of the most important cultural issues of our day. And it is a subject which has aroused significant controversy within the church. It is a subject which has stirred questions within the Reformed Presbyterian Church of North America (RPCNA). Although we are only one denomination among many, we have endeavored to respond faithfully to these questions as they have arisen in our midst, examining them prayerfully and pastorally in local, presbytery, and synod assemblies.

After several years of this process of deliberation within the courts of the RPCNA, we are now prepared to offer our conclusions in writing. At the Synod of 2011, this document was unanimously adopted as a denominational testimony on the Gospel and sexual orientation. We now offer it in print for the instruction of our own congregations, for the edification and review of sister denominations, and as an aspect of our united Gospel witness to the world.

Contemporary questions about sexual orientation are not simple, and they must not be treated simplistically. There are sophisticated medical, scientific, theological, and exegetical arguments at issue in the present controversy. In order to treat such arguments seriously, this book is written with a degree of scholarly earnest. But do not let the theological rigor of the book hinder you from appreciating its pastoral heart. The study contained in this book was first undertaken to help particular people with specific questions on the subject. It was not written in a vacuum of theory, but in the midst of face-to-face dialogue and prayer with real people. It is now being published with that same concern to reach people with needs and questions (it is not published for ivory tower debate). Therefore, while the meat of the book necessarily treats weighty matters of theology and science, the final chapter of the book applies the study's conclusions in points of practical guidance.

It would be impossible to acknowledge all who contributed to this book. The following are those who served on the two study committees behind its preparation: on the 2009 Study Committee of the Great Lakes–Gulf Presbytery, James Faris (chairman), Keith Magill, and Michael LeFebvre; on the 2010 RPCNA Synod Study Committee, Michael LeFebvre (chairman), Ken Smith, Howard Huizing, Rich Holdeman, and Zachary Kail. However, this study has benefitted from valuable input from many pastors and laymen, both inside the RPCNA and outside, some with personal experience in same-sex struggles and others with ministry experience in these areas. To list all their names is not possible, and we thank them all.

We offer this book to you with prayer it will be edifying to your soul as well as informative to your understanding. Most of all, we pray that this testimony will bring help and encouragement to many who need the Gospel of Jesus Christ, and that his name will be glorified.

—*Michael LeFebvre, February 2012,*
chairperson of Reformed Presbyterian Church of North America's
study committee on "Perspectives on Sexual Orientation."

I

Introduction and Terminology

The word *homosexuality* was originally coined in German (*Homosexualität*) in 1869 by Karl-Maria Kertbeny. Kertbeny, an Austrian-born social reformer, first introduced the term in a pamphlet written to oppose the adoption of Prussian anti-sodomy laws in the new constitution for the unified German state then being formed.[1] The new term was quickly adopted in German discourse, and was brought into English in 1892.[2] Other European societies followed suit and, by the early 20th century, medical experts and law-makers across western Europe and North America were moving away from older terms like *sodomy* to use the new word, *homosexuality*.

But the old word (*sodomy*) and new word (*homosexuality*) are not equivalents. The shift in terminology was not simply a change of words; it was part of a broader shift in how same-sex issues were coming to be understood. Rather than viewing a person who engages in same-sex activity as acting against

---

[1] Karl-Maria Kertbeny (originally published anonymously), *Paragraph 143 of the Prussian Penal Code of 14 April 1851 and Its Reaffirmation as Paragraph 152 in the Proposed Penal Code for the North German Confederation. An Open and Professional Correspondence to His Excellency Dr. Leonhardt, Royal Prussian Minister of Justice* (Leipzig: Serbe's Verlag, 1869). Note that Kertbeny formed the word *homosexuality* by combining the Greek *homo* (meaning "same"; not the Latin *homo*, meaning "man") with the Latin *sexualis* (meaning "sex").

[2] When Charles Gilbert Chaddock translated Richard von Krafft-Ebing's 1886, *Psychopathia Sexualis,* into English.

the way he or she is "sexually wired" (and thus labeled a *sodomite*) it was now argued that some people are actually physiologically "wired," sexually, for same-sex desires (and thus are, by nature, *homosexual*).

Some advocates of this new perspective offer the example of a person's handedness as an analogy.[3] Most people are right-handed; the number of people who are left-handed has always been a minority. As a result, often throughout history, society has been prejudiced against left-handed individuals. For instance, an awkward dancer is said to have "two left feet" (why not "two right feet"?) and, in some societies, efforts have been made to retrain left-handed children to give prominence to their right hands. There is no biblical doctrine that exalts either left or right handedness as innately superior; however, there have been prejudices against left-handedness through history, because it is a minority orientation. Modern science has confirmed, however, that handedness is not a matter of choice nor something which children should be "trained out of." While most people are naturally "wired" for right-handedness (roughly 9 out of 10 people are right-handed), some are actually genetically pre-disposed to left-handedness. In 2007, a group of scientists identified the gene (called LRRTM1) which disposes a person to left-handedness.[4] According to the proponents of the new perspective on same-sex issues, a re-characterization of sexual orientation along similar lines is required. Same-sex desires are, they argue, not a matter of moral choices, but are a natural disposition—a legitimate sexual identity. Words like *sodomy, sodomite, sexual perversion,* and so forth, reflect the traditional presupposition that same-sex activity is a perversion of a person's natural gender role. The term *homosexual* (along with its counterpart, *heterosexual*) was coined to convey the new idea that some people are same-sex oriented by nature and ought not be prejudiced against simply because it is a minority orientation.

Certainly, even those promoting this new perspective continue to recognize that there are some individuals who engage in same-sex activities due to their circumstances and not due to any inner orientation. For instance, men who lust for sexual stimulation but who are confined in situations where no female companionship is possible (as in some military situations or in

---

[3] Chandler Burr, "Homosexuality and Biology," 132–3; in, *Homosexuality in the Church: Both Sides of the Debate* (Jeffrey S. Siker, ed.; Louisville: Westminster John Knox, 1994), 116–34.

[4] *Molecular Psychiatry* 12 (2007), 1129–1139.

prison), sometimes turn to same-sex sex against their natural orientation. Such cases continue to be identified by behavioral terms, like *sodomy* or *pederasty*. However, the word *homosexuality* was designed to refer to those for whom same-sex interests are believed to emerge from the individual's "true" sexual identity. The *GLBTQ Encyclopedia* explains,

> Homosexuality and heterosexuality emerged as concepts in late nineteenth-century European medical and juridical discourse. Their introduction and popularization occasioned a revolution in the way sexual behavior was understood by linking that behavior inextricably to social identity, hastening cultural changes in the organization of sexuality already underway in urban areas of Europe and North America.[5]

This shift in understanding has major implications for the church. Yet unfortunately, while there are numerous statements from Reformed and presbyterian denominations addressing same-sex *practices* and same-sex *desires*, there are few ecclesiastical papers dealing specifically with the question of "homosexual *orientation*."[6] We believe this is a subject that needs to be examined and addressed by the church. We hope that this paper will contribute toward greater understanding among churches striving to respond to questions about homosexuality and to reach out to those who experience same-sex desires.

There are several aspects of the "homosexuality as an orientation" paradigm that need to be confronted. First of all, this new claim raises a profound challenge to the traditional understanding of the doctrine of man, specifically in relation to human sexuality and gender as part of mankind's reflection of God's likeness. Either the church's traditional understanding of genders and sexual identity needs to be corrected to accommodate the new perspectives on homosexuality, or the church's traditional positions on these matters need to be re-articulated in ways that show their relevance to the modern claims (see Chapters II–III).

---

[5] "Homosexuality," *GLBTQ Encyclopedia: Social Sciences* (www.glbtq.com/social-sciences/homosexuality.html; accessed 12/28/2009).

[6] E.g., the statements of NAPARC churches at the following web addresses: *OPC statement*—www.opc.org/GA/homosexuality.html; *PCA summary of statements*—www.alliancenet.org/partner/Article_Display_Page/0,,PTID23682_CHID125044_CIID1620134,00.html; *ARP statement*—www.arpsynod.org/position.html; *EPC statement*—www.epc.org/about-the-epc/position-papers/homosexuality; (accessed 01/29/2010.)

Secondly, there is extensive exegetical work being done by biblical scholars revisiting the biblical texts on *sodomy* and how (indeed, whether) they speak to issues of *homosexuality*. The church needs to keep her doctrines on same-sex issues grounded in careful exegesis with discernment as to the hermeneutical presuppositions that give rise to various counter-interpretations (see Chapters IV–V). Finally, because these are issues touching on the lives of real people in deep and profound ways, the church's treatment of these theological questions must bear the fruits of pastoral direction for ministering to those with same-sex attractions. Indeed, there has never before in history been such an immense amount of research into the nature of same-sex issues, and while the church's theological stance may not be changed by this research, pastorally there is much that can be learned from recent research for better understanding and ministering to "homosexuals" in our communities (see Chapter VI).

II

Biology, Gender, and the Biblical Doctrine of Man

For millennia, same-sex behavior has been viewed as a moral perversion deserving heaven's judgment. In the biblical account of Sodom and Gomorrah, where the same-sex demands of the men of Sodom against Lot's guests were answered by a downfall of literal hellfire and brimstone, the church historically found a most awful warning against such violations of proper sexual order, and society in general found a name for it—*sodomy.*

As noted above, the introduction of new terminology (*homosexuality,* followed by other neutral terms like *gay, lesbian, bisexual, transgender, queer*) reflects a change in the way society has come to regard same-sex attractions. Rather than linking them to moral failures, it is now posited that sociological or physiological factors cause this sexual orientation. By breaking with tradition and positing a different cause for a "same-sex orientation," modern science has also set up for itself a need to demonstrate and identify just exactly what the social or physiological cause for homosexual orientation is. Once the theory was provided, scientific research to test and prove the theory has followed in earnest.

Through much of the early century of this research, psychiatry led the way looking for *social* influences which might cause homosexual orientation. In fact, until 1973 homosexuality was listed in the American Psychiatric Association's *Diagnostic and Statistical Manual of Mental Disorders* (DSM) as a psychiatric condition. However, decades of psychiatric research to identify social or cultural factors for the condition produced few convincing results. Furthermore, since studies of homosexual men and women found that they were otherwise well adapted mentally and socially, it was determined that regarding it as a psychiatric *pathology* was heading in the wrong direction.[7] As Chandler Burr explains, "Psychiatry had succeeded in defining what homosexuality is *not*— not in explaining what it is. Questions of etiology…thus became by default questions for neurobiology."[8]

In the last few decades, biology has been at the forefront of the question, looking for the "gay gene" or brain structures associated with sexual orientation. Biologists had already been interested in studying structural differences between the brains of men and women. Such studies of gender differences in the brain were now expanded to compare anatomical features in the brains of "heterosexual" and "homosexual" individuals, with related experiments on laboratory animals. Several decades of this pursuit for the "gay gene"—or other evidence for "sexual orientation" in the brain—has produced many intriguing insights (and lots of impassioned claims on all sides); however, definitive results remain unclear. In a recent (May 2009) pamphlet on the subject from the American Psychological Association, the state of the scientific community is summarized thus:

> Although much research has examined the possible genetic, hormonal, developmental, social, and cultural influences on sexual orientation, no findings have emerged that permit scientists to conclude that sexual orientation is determined by any particular factor or factors. Many think that nature and nurture both play complex roles…[9]

It would be easy to misread this statement as suggesting no evidence at all has been found for "homosexual orientation."[10] That is not the result that

---

[7] E.g., Evelyn Hooker, "The Adjustment of the Male Overt Homosexual," in, *The Problem of Homosexuality in Modern Society* (H. M. Ruitenbeeck, ed.; New York: Dutton, 1963), 141–61.

[8] Chandler Burr, "Homosexuality and Biology," 120.

[9] "Answers to Your Questions For a Better Understanding of Sexual Orientation & Homosexuality" (www.apa.org/topics/sexuality/orientation.aspx; accessed 12/28/2009).

[10] Some conservative voices have latched onto the apparent failure of modern science to provide a "smoking gun" demonstration of such physiological causation as indication

scientists are giving to us; the scientific community has not abandoned the claim that same-sex desires emerge from something deeper in a person than his or her own, personal choices. Too many of those who wrestle with these desires experience them from early childhood and in ways that seem, to researchers, to confirm the presence of causes deeper than personal, moral choices. However, the last century of research has indicated that finding a single, "smoking gun" cause (e.g., a single "gay gene") is unlikely. It is now generally believed, as indicated in the APA statement above, that sexual orientation develops out of some kind of a "perfect storm" of both natural (e.g., genetic or *in utero* chemical) and social (e.g., childhood or developmental) influences. Of course, the conclusions of the scientific community are in constant flux, and one can never be certain where future research will lead. But what is the church's response to this developing (and ever-changing) body of scientific material to be?

We believe the church should welcome the insights of scientific studies in this field. There is no reason to deny the helpfulness of the perspectives offered by such research. At the same time, we also believe such insights should be received with a measured degree of caution. A degree of skepticism should be maintained about contemporary research into sexual orientation questions, for at least two reasons.

First, the whole endeavor is rooted in the presupposition that there are physiological causes for every human tendency. That is, the scientific community today has, for the most part, adopted the presupposition that man is a material being without any immaterial soul. What we call the "soul" in man is, according to contemporary thought, simply an expression of physical and chemical (that is, material) reactions. Therefore, from the very beginning of the scientific community's search for causes of same-sex desires, a physiological solution is expected. The APA statement quoted earlier interprets the lack of clear evidence for a particular, naturalistic cause for same-sex desires as indicating that there must therefore be a complex "perfect storm" of causation. However, the reason for this conclusion is because a materialist view of man presupposes that some physiological cause must exist. We simply note that this materialist presupposition is not, itself, without its critics within the scientific

---

that the whole hypothesis is in error. E.g., A. Dean Byrd, "APA's New Pamphlet on Homosexuality De-emphasizes the Biological Argument, Supports a Client's Right to Self-Determination" (www.narth.com/docs/deemphasizes.html; accessed 12/28/2008).

community;[11] and it certainly is not a presupposition from which we as the church can work (cf., *Westminster Confession of Faith [WCF]* 4.2; *Westminster Larger Catechism [WLC]* 86). On the contrary, we believe that the failure of the scientific community to identify a clear causation for this orientation may actually suggest that the presupposed materialism behind the endeavor is ill-grounded.

Second, we could wish that there was more objectivity and less politically motivated pressure behind the scientific community's work in this field. The presence of so much political and lobbying pressure to prove the validity of same-sex *orientation* makes it difficult for theologians, who are generally not experts in scientific matters, to know what published research to trust and what is not trustworthy. Ronald Bayer notes, for instance, that the 1973 vote by the APA to remove *homosexuality* from the *DSM* list of pathologies took place under pressure from disruptive demonstrations and threats from gay rights groups. Based on a follow-up survey of APA members conducted after the vote, Bayer concludes that the majority of members actually held opinions opposite to the turnout of the vote and that the decision, therefore, "might have been affected by sociopolitical considerations."[12] We certainly are not in a position to review such events, but simply recall that even scientific consensus is not formed in a vacuum, and the immense political pressure in this field introduces an unavoidable degree of wariness. Many of those involved in the quest, as the proponents themselves admit, have a personal interest in proving its existence (being themselves "homosexuals").[13] Furthermore, as noted at the head of this paper, the effort to recognize a homosexual orientation was originally launched as part of a *social reform* movement in Germany. For all of these various reasons, it is hard for us to avoid the concern that at least some of the work in this field continues to be motivated more by social reform agendas than by a truly objective (i.e., scientific) concern to understand same-sex desires, as though the traditional concern to help reform the one struggling with same-sex desires (rather than reforming society's understandings of gender and sexual identities) is conclusively incorrect.

---

[11] E.g., Mario Beauregard and Denyse O'Leary, *The Spiritual Brain: A Neuroscientist's Case for the Existence of the Soul* (New York: HarperOne, 2007).

[12] Ronald Bayer, *Homosexuality and American Psychiatry: The Politics of Diagnosis* [New York: Basic Books, 1981], 167.

[13] E.g., Chandler Burr, "Homosexuality and Biology," 117, 131.

With these concerns being voiced, we nonetheless do believe that the church should willingly engage with the insights which scientific research is offering—even if we do not believe that the church should feel compelled to adopt this widely held hypothesis, yet. The evidence for this conclusion (that same-sex desires are caused by a genetic orientation) is still too weak to be regarded as conclusive. We still have to consider, however, whether it is *biblically sound* to allow that an innate homosexual orientation might one day be demonstrated; and, if so, whether such a finding would require the church to reform her doctrine of man in any substantial way.

While we admit the aforementioned points of skepticism, we nonetheless do not believe it is beyond the bounds of a biblical view of man to allow that some innate "cause(s)" for same-sex desires could be defined. However—and this is a crucial point—the implications of such a finding for the church would be primarily pastoral, not theological. That is, if this modern paradigm of sexual orientation is proven correct, this does not warrant a change in the church's doctrines in any substantial manner. Contrary to the claims of liberal churchman and the assumptions of many scientists, that such a scientific finding would require the church to change its theological-ethical stance toward same-sex issues, we believe such a finding would valuably inform the church's compassion and her ministry to those experiencing this "orientation;" however, the biblical doctrine of man (including human sexuality) as historically confessed by the church would not be "re-written" by such a finding.

Chandler Burr is a gay author who illustrates the position of churches seeking to legitimize homosexuality. Mr. Burr is best known for his book on *The Search for the Biological Origins of Sexual Orientation*, which was published by a Disney subsidiary (Hyperion) in 1996 and prompted the widely publicized boycott of Disney by Southern Baptists. Mr. Burr illustrates the posture of many in churches today when he poses the question: If sexual orientation is found to be biologically determined (as he is persuaded it will), "How can one justify discriminating against people on the basis of such a characteristic?... God made gay people this way...[and] like it or not..., there are majority and minority expressions of [sexuality]..."[14] Similarly, Dan O. Via, professor emeritus of New Testament at Duke University Divinity School, writes, "We do not know for certain whether homosexual orientation is essential (biological

---

[14] Chandler Burr, "Homosexuality and Biology," 132–3.

and genetic) or constructed (psychological and social) or both; but whatever is the case, even some who hold very strongly to the traditional view agree that at least some part of the gay population is immutably [i.e., unchangeably] so… Should then homosexual orientation not be considered a different sexual order of creation, the actualization of which in practice would be natural?"[15]

It is widely believed by such advocates that, if homosexuality is shown to have biological and/or sociological causes (thereby *proving* the "homosexual orientation" hypothesis), that this would be indication that *homosexuality is part of God's natural order*. However, this conclusion would not follow, of necessity, from such proof. While we believe that such discoveries would have significant implications for understanding and pastoring men and women with these struggles, an orthodox understanding of Scripture, and particularly its teaching on the effects of original sin upon human nature, do not support the logic of men like Burr and Via.

In chapter 6 of the *Westminster Confession of Faith*, we confess that,

> By [Adam's] sin, [our first parents] fell from their original righteousness and communion with God, and so became dead in sin, *and wholly defiled in all the parts and faculties of soul and body*. They being the root of all mankind, the guilt of this sin was imputed, *and the same death in sin and corrupted nature conveyed* to all their posterity, descending from them by ordinary generation. (*WCF* 6.2–3).

Sexual identity is included in the "all parts and faculties of soul and body" which have been disordered by original sin. Genesis teaches us that the created sexual order, which God pronounced objectively "very good," (Gen. 1:31), involves two genders, sexually designed for one another. "God created man … male and female," and when God brought the woman to the man, the man declared, "This at last is bone of my bones and flesh of my flesh…" The inspired theologian who recorded this event gives us its doctrinal implications, stating, "Therefore a man shall leave his father and his mother and hold fast to his wife, and they shall become one flesh" (Gen. 1:27; 2:23–24). That this teaching of Genesis 1–2 is specifically about the sexual identity of the male and female for each other (and not simply using the man and woman as examples

---

[15] Dan O. Via, "The Bible, the Church, and Homosexuality," 32, 35; in, Dan O. Via and Robert A. J. Gagnon, *Homosexuality and the Bible: Two Views* (Minneapolis: Fortress Press, 2003), 1–39.

of all kinds of loving, sexual relationships) is confirmed by subsequent passages throughout Scripture, which identify other "orientations" of sexuality as corruptions of this one-man-and-one-woman creation order, including fornication (e.g., Deut. 22:28–29), adultery (e.g., Deut. 22:22), polygamy (e.g., Gen. 4:19; 1 Tim. 3:2), bestiality (e.g., Ex. 22:19), prostitution (e.g., Lev. 19:29), incest (e.g., Lev. 18:6), cross-dressing (e.g., Deut. 22:5), and same-sex intercourse (e.g., Lev. 18:22; 20:13).[16]

Many of these alternate sexual orientations (both the desires and the associated behaviors) may genuinely have deeper and more complicated factors influencing those who are tempted by them than simple "free will" decisions. In fact, taking a cue from the last century of work to tie same-sex desires to natural causes, recent studies on "zoophilia" are positing similar biological sources for an in-born orientation toward sex with animals.[17] (*Zoophilia* is the term which has now been coined to represent the purported sexual orientation behind animal-sex desires as an alternative to the old behavioristic term *bestiality*.) Are we to discover that there are biological underpinnings to all manner of sexual orientations, including group sex and animal sex and so on? While skeptical concerning the validity of such claims (for reasons stated earlier), we nonetheless do not outright deny the *possibility* that biological influences for even these other "orientations" (such as polygamy or "zoophilia" and so on) *might* be found. The present condition of human nature is, as Scripture teaches us, disordered from its proper design, and the true depth of its brokenness is undoubtedly beyond our comprehension (Jer. 17:9). However, we confess with Scripture that the creation order which God pronounced to be objectively "good," before human nature became burdened with many lusts and confusions of all kinds, constitutes two genders that are sexually oriented for one another. If science shows us that sexual disorders are more deeply enmeshed in human biology than the church has traditionally understood, this ought to stir our concern for even greater understanding and compassion for those who experience these desires; however, it does not change the fact that such inclinations are contrary to human nature as God designed it—and as he is redeeming it.

---

[16] Cf., pp. 43–45.

[17] E.g., Hani Miletski, *Understanding Bestiality & Zoophilia*. (Bethesda, Md.: East-West Publishing, 2002).

As Greg Bahnsen explains,

Even if it were somehow shown that this idea [that some are born with a homosexual predisposition] has biblical warrant, this fact would not lead in itself to the conclusion that the individual who has a distinctive sinful bent (say, toward homosexuality) in his inherited depraved nature is somehow less personally responsible for the corresponding desires and acts than for other sinful desires and acts. Adherents of the view in question have to show biblical support for the idea that the individual cannot be held specifically responsible for those particular sins that are *ingrained* in his depraved nature ... Everyone must recognize that original sin ... is itself sinful in character and something for which its inheritors are held personally culpable (Rom. 5:12, 15–19) ... The present theory contributes nothing to an ethical evaluation of homosexuality."[18]

Same-sex *behavior* is identified in Scripture as an "offense" (תּוֹעֵבָה) against God's sexual order (Lev. 18:22) and same-sex *inclinations* are also identified as "dishonorable passions" (πάθη ἀτιμίας; Rom. 1:26–27).[19] What the findings of modern science might be telling us is that such desires, where experienced, are more deeply tied to the effects of original sin than we may often have recognized. Sometimes a person brings upon him/herself same-sex experiences that stir up same-sex desires. However, perhaps in a greater number of cases than we have tended to appreciate, these desires were not deliberately sought out, and the self-blame and intense sense of guilt that many experience simply over *having* these struggles needs to be compassionately addressed. There truly may be those who struggle with same-sex temptations, not due to any particular choices of their own, but because of the brokenness of human nature. However, the church's doctrine of human nature, and our understanding of gender and sexual morality, remain anchored in the teachings of Scripture, which already provide an explanation for even biological disorders in "all parts and faculties of soul and body."

Frankly, a deep-seated propensity to same-sex desires would certainly not be the only (or even the most difficult) kind of brokenness to bear. As Stanton Jones and Don Workman point out, "An adult child of an alcoholic *may* have

---

[18] Greg L. Bahnsen, *Homosexuality: A Biblical View* (Grand Rapids: Baker, 1978), 70.

[19] See the exegesis of these passages in Chapter V.

a biological predisposition [to excessive drink]"—a physiological disorder experienced because of one's parents.[20] Similarly, many people struggle with mental health disorders like depression or schizophrenia or ADHD, which (we are told by medical experts) can also have biological factors beyond the individual's control. We are certainly not suggesting that a sexual struggle is comparable to a mental disorder or alcoholic tendencies. However, these and other common afflictions of mankind remind us that each of us, in different ways, share in the impact of someone else's sin as well as our own: Adam's in particular, as well as the sins of others whose lives intersect with ours. Furthermore, each of these afflictions leave a person more vulnerable to certain sins than those with different afflictions. For example, if indeed ADHD has biological factors, a person with this condition is more prone to distraction and boredom with his work, may find it more difficult to pay attention to the words of his wife, and (we are told) may be more prone to blurt out what is on his mind. There are moral implications for such tendencies, and a man with ADHD would not cease to be morally responsible because of these tendencies. He simply would need to realize that he, perhaps on account of biological or sociological influences that are the result of original sin, is more vulnerable to certain temptations and must, with great humility and prayer and full exercise of the means of grace, take hope in the promises of redemption for every part of the body and soul while striving to honor the image of God in his own life. The other examples mentioned, depression and schizophrenia, are likewise matters of much controversy and debate regarding their purported biological origin. However those questions are resolved, they illustrate conditions which, in some cases (like schizophrenia), may even be more difficult to bear than struggling with same-sex desires.

Perhaps we will find, in coming generations, that the tendency of modern science to trace so many human experiences (physically and psychologically) to biological influences is a fad which will ultimately be more severely qualified. Perhaps future scientists will look back on our era and see that our fascination with functional MRIs and DNA-mapping and other (for us) groundbreaking technologies were over-hyped in what they were really telling us. We might recall, for instance, some of the tragic results of lobotomies performed in

---

[20] Stanton L. Jones and Don E. Workman, "Homosexuality: The Behavioral Sciences and the Church," 106.

the mid-20th century due to the inflated conclusions of early brain-mapping research.[21] Perhaps in future generations, it will be found that the sexual orientation hypotheses of our age, as well as neurological "causes" of various mental disorders, eating disorders, and so forth, while associated with real findings, are similarly over-rated in the meaning of those findings. We may find that these conclusions are too heavily shaped by the presupposition of current science that all human conditions have *material* causes, and we may one day come to realize that the biological features identified for certain conditions are not really causes but simply coordinate expressions of something with an even deeper, non-biological, origin. But it is also possible that future science will more thoroughly demonstrate that the biological factors associated with such conditions truly are causative. It may even be found that there is a "gay gene," so that even homosexuality is congenital. The answers to these questions are extremely important; however, they do not in themselves call for a reform of the church's historic doctrine of man, of human sexuality, and the impact of original sin.

In fact, while it has often been claimed that the Bible provides no treatment of socially or biologically influenced homosexuality (and only speaks of personal choices), we believe that Paul's descriptions in Romans 1 are far more insightful on these matters than some have given credit. In that chapter, Paul is not talking about an *individual's* decline into sin through personal choices and behaviors; he moves systematically in that chapter through a description of how a *society* declines from one level of folly (vv. 18–23) into dishonorable lusts (vv. 24–25) and then into dishonorable passions (including same-sex temptations; vv. 26–27) and finally, if there is no repentance, to a "debased mind" (vv. 28–32). We don't believe Paul is necessarily providing a mechanical description of a precise sequence of steps through which a society degenerates, but he is providing a typical description of *a culture's* decline. His use of the plural pronouns throughout that passage, and his application of this chapter to communities (Jewish and Gentile) in the subsequent chapters, indicate that he is not describing the decline of one individual through various temptations because of his own sins alone. Thus, even the context of Paul's reference to same-sex desires in Romans 1 should be a reminder to us (and to those who

---

[21] Cf., Hernish J. Acharya, "The Rise and Fall of the Frontal Lobotomy," in, *Proceedings of the 13th Annual History of Medicine Days* (W. A. Whitelaw, ed.; Calgary: Faculty of Medicine, University of Calgary, 2004), 32–41.

struggle with this temptation) that the human race is a community in which we each bear the scars of others' sins, not merely our own.[22] Within that context, the Apostle Paul himself points to "dishonorable passions" in one generation as the fruits of the sinfulness of society in past generations. Certainly Paul had no concept of genetic or biological issues that might naturalistically communicate the effects of sin from one generation to another, but he clearly recognize that the corruption which individuals wrestle with in many aspects of human nature have more complex causes than the simplistic outlook of Job's counselors.

Even in the century prior to modern notions about sexual orientation, Jonathan Edwards was already writing about the roots of many sins in the "natural constitution" (i.e., the "orientation") of a person. In his "Treatise on Religious Affections," Edwards wrote with keen discernment and pastoral sensitivity about such "constitutional" struggles:

> Allowances, indeed, must be made for the natural temper, which conversion does not entirely eradicate: those sins which a man by his natural constitution was most inclined to before his conversion, he may be most apt to fall into still. But yet conversion will make a great alteration even with respect to these sins. Though grace, while imperfect, does not root out an evil natural temper, yet it is of great power and efficacy to correct it. The change wrought in conversion, is an universal change: grace changes a man with respect to whatever is sinful in him; the *old man* is put off, and the *new man* put on; he is sanctified throughout. He is become a new creature, old things are passed away, and *all things* are become new; all sin is mortified, constitutional sins, as well as others. If a man before his conversion was, by his natural constitution, prone to lasciviousness, or drunkenness, or maliciousness; converting grace will make a great alteration in him, with respect to these evil dispositions; so that however he may be still most in danger of these sins, they shall no longer have dominion over him; nor will they any more be properly his character. Yes, true repentance, in some respects especially, turns a man against his *own* iniquity; *that* wherein he has been most guilty, and has chiefly dishonoured God. He that forsakes other sins, but preserves the iniquity to which he is chiefly inclined, is like Saul, who, when sent

[22] Cf., Richard B. Hays, "Awaiting the Redemption of Our Bodies: The Witness of Scripture Concerning Homosexuality," 7–9; in, *Homosexuality in the Church* (Jeffrey S. Siker, ed.), 3–17; Greg L. Bahnsen, *Homosexuality: A Biblical View*, 68.

against God's enemies the Amalekites, with a strict charge to save none of them alive, but utterly to destroy them, small and great; slew the people, but saved the king.[23]

While neither the biblical writers (like Paul) nor later theologians (like Jonathan Edwards) were aware of modern theories about sexual orientation, they were not naïve concerning the role of a person's unchosen, natural disposition in the particular temptations and sins with which that individual will struggle.

To summarize this important point: even if it were to be demonstrated beyond reasonable doubt that some people possess a same-sex orientation through biological or sociological factors outside their own control, this would not indicate that homosexuality is part of God's intended order. It would (and, even at the current provisional stage of the scientific findings in this realm, ought to) increase our awareness of how desperate the human condition is, how utterly hopeless men are of achieving renewal simply by self-will or behaviorism, and, frankly, how imbalanced the effects of sin are throughout human experience that some people experience one area of brokenness more deeply while other people experience another more heavily.

We recognize that this doctrine of sin, and of human nature's "total depravity" because of sin, is a very depressing doctrine, and one which seems unfair and full of hopelessness by itself. But indeed, that is the tragic nature of sin and the curse as taught by Scripture. In every age, it is the church's responsibility to bring this sad truth to bear on the conditions of that generation. It is also the reason why the Apostle Paul, with his own experiences of brokenness, cried out, "I delight in the law of God in my inner being, but I see in my members another law waging war against the law of my mind and making me captive to the law of sin that dwells in my members. Wretched man that I am! Who will deliver me from this body of death? *Thanks be to God through Jesus Christ our Lord!...*" (Rom. 7:22–25). Only after sharing in Paul's understanding of the true hopelessness of our broken condition, right down to that agonizing tension of one's own conflicted, inner desires so often testified by those who experience same-sex temptations, can we also realize how glorious the hope of redemption is which Paul leads us in championing with his exultant cry amidst his struggles: "Thanks be to God

---

[23] Jonathan Edwards, "A Treatise Concerning Religious Affections, in Three Parts," Part 3, chapter 7.

through Jesus Christ our Lord!" The bondage and afflictions of the curse really do run that deep; but it is against the backdrop of such struggles that the profound power and immeasurable greatness of God's grace shines forth with splendor and stirs our hearts with a yearning for sanctification and hope in heaven. In the face of such real and even uncontrollable inclinations, our desperate need for a Redeemer who is truly a powerful Savior (not merely a wise teacher) becomes a focus of our longing and our joy.

Through life, *every* person will face profound struggles sexually, whether those temptations be "heterosexual" or "homosexual." We think for instance of the many Christians who find themselves married to a spouse who is no longer sexually satisfying perhaps for legitimate reasons (such as a sexually disabling illness on the part of the other spouse), and thus find themselves in a position to honor God with their sexuality with intense difficulty. "Homosexual" men and women are not the only ones called to honor God's design for human sexuality in the face of extremely difficult pressures. And admittedly, such struggles are not "fairly" distributed, so that the church needs to learn to provide particular encouragement to those struggling with some of the heavier forms of sexual temptation such as same-sex desires. Nonetheless, the church's proclamation has been reduced to "self-help" mantras if we do not recognize that there are aspects of human brokenness that really are beyond our ability to "fix" ourselves, yet which still require faith, prayer, and waiting upon the mercy of the Savior to redeem.

While left-handedness and right-handedness are examples of biological orientations which have no moral consequences (there is nothing sinful about writing with one hand or the other), a same-sex orientation (if biologically caused) does have moral consequences. As deeply enmeshed in the soul or body as modern thought posits it to be, same-sex desires call for faith in a powerful Savior who created us male and female, and who can be trusted to truly redeem his people "in all the parts and faculties of soul and body"—even if he does not always complete our redemption on the schedule that we long for, or even, in his wisdom, within this lifetime. That kind of trust is what faith (and faithful obedience) is all about.

Some theologians today lean too heavily on those scientists who insist that the "homosexual orientation" is immutable and cannot be changed or healed.[24]

---

[24] E.g., the quotation of Dan O. Via on p. 14.

Even this claim of immutability is controversial, however. Some researchers do report successes in "re-orienting" same-sex desires.[25] Furthermore, even if in some cases the desires are so deeply ingrained (and even innately "caused"), so that reform truly is humanly impossible, it is not the experience of such individuals that defines the "new nature" into which Jesus is patiently (sometimes too patiently, it seems to us) renewing his people. In all points of our Christian struggles, Scripture teaches us to see our "true selves" as being found in the "new man" which is after the likeness of Christ (cf., the nature of man as created in Gen. 1–2), and not in the experiences of our "old man" wrestlings (Eph. 4:17–24). Without denying or belittling the intense, seemingly irresolvable struggle that same-sex desires genuinely entail for many men and women, the testimony of Scripture is clear: "…neither the sexually immoral, nor idolaters, nor adulterers, nor men who practice homosexuality… *And such were some of you. But you were washed, you were sanctified, you were justified in the name of the Lord Jesus Christ and by the Spirit of our God*" (1 Cor. 6:9–11). It is the nature of the Spirit's transforming power to address even the deepest struggles of the human soul and to bring the power of the resurrection to bear upon them.

---

[25] E.g., the various studies reviewed by Stanton L. Jones and Don E. Workman, "Homosexuality: The Behavioral Sciences and the Church," 103–4; in, *Homosexuality in the Church* (Jeffrey S. Siker, ed.), 93–115, as well as the extensive study completed by Stanton L. Jones and Mark A. Yarhouse, *Ex-Gays? A Longitudinal Study of Religiously Mediated Change in Sexual Orientation* (Downers Grove, Ill.: InterVarsity Press, 2007).

III

Personality Traits and the Multiplication of Gender Categories

One of the sexual reformers in 19th century Germany (and an early proponent of the new terminology) was a man named Karl Heinrich Ulrichs. In his writings and speeches on homosexuality, Ulrichs famously spoke of himself as "*anima muliebris virili corpore inclusa*" ("a female soul confined by a male body").[26] Ulrichs was careful to qualify his statement, admitting that he saw in himself *some* typically female traits and *some* typically male traits;[27] nevertheless, the large number of traits he found in himself which are commonly associated with women added to his sense that his "identity" was something other than that of a male. In addition to his same-sex desires, Ulrichs pointed to these feminine qualities to his personality as indication that he was oriented differently than a typical man, thus justifying what essentially amounts to a new gender category: homosexual.

Ulrichs popularized a perception that is carried on today in the colloquial expression, "sex is between the legs and gender is between the ears," and in the scientific fields of research into the neurological bases, not only for "sexual orientation," but also for "brain gender." Since homosexuality is generally

---

[26] E.g., the title page of his *Memnon. Die Geschlechtsnatur des mannliebenden Urnings. Eine naturwissen-schaftliche Darstellung.* (Schleiz: Hübscher, 1868).

[27] Karl Heinrich Ulrichs, *Memnon*, 115–16, cited in, Hubert Kennedy, *Karl Heinrich Ulrichs: Pioneer of the Modern Gay Movement* (San Francisco: Peremptory Publications, 2002), 154.

identified based on both same-sex desires *and* what is called "gender-role non-conformity,"[28] we believe it is also important to address these new trends in defining one's "brain gender." Once our society adopted the "sexual orientation" hypothesis, our entire concept of human gender has become confused. According to one classification system representative of this modern confusion, every individual has:

(1) a *biological sex* (male, female, or intersex) which is determined by one's physical anatomy;

(2) a *gender identity* (which can be masculine, feminine, or transgender) which is based on how a person acts, talks, dresses, and behaves in relation to the gender norms established by society; and

(3) a *sexual orientation* (which can be heterosexual, homosexual, or bisexual) which based on one's sexual attractions.[29]

That is, a person might have, for instance, the body of a man (biological sex), the brain of a woman (gender identity), and the sexual orientation of both (bisexual). While considering a person's sexuality, mental traits, and physique in distinct categories might be an interesting way to make categorizations about various aspects of an individual's personality *in the laboratory,* it is troubling that these categories are being given the weight of *literal* new gender categories. We confess, biblically, that God created human beings as male or female, with sexual orientation *and* gender identity being one and the same as that individual's biological sex. We have already considered the sameness of one's *biological sex* and proper *sexual orientation* in previous sections of the paper; it is the middle category, *gender identity* (allegedly determined by a person's mannerisms and other gender-typical or non-typical traits) that needs to be addressed next.

It has been common, all through history, to speak about "masculine traits" and "feminine traits" based on generalizations of human experience. For a recent example, John Gray's bestseller, *Men Are from Mars, Women Are from Venus,* is built around the discussion of such generalizations as the following:

"Men…offer solutions…while women offer unsolicited advice…"

"While [men] tend to pull away and silently think about what's bothering

---

[28] "Homosexuality," *GLBTQ Encyclopedia: Social Sciences* (www.glbtq.com/social-sciences/homosexuality.html; accessed 12/28/2009).

[29] (www.plannedparenthood.org/health-topics/sexual-orientation-gender-4329.htm; accessed: 12/28/2009).

them, [women] feel an instinctive need to talk about what's bothering them."

"Men are motivated when they feel needed while women are motivated when they feel cherished."

[Regarding sexual intimacy,] "A man gets close but then inevitably needs to pull away... A woman's loving attitudes rise and fall rhythmically in a wave motion."[30]

This way of classifying personality traits along gender lines has become a popular theme in Christian marriage books, as well. There is nothing wrong with such generalizations, so long as we are careful not to become overly dogmatic that certain sets of traits are the inherent property of one gender or the other. Such generalizations are no more than that: generalizations based on the kinds of traits which *often* appear in men or in women, respectively. A careful consideration of an individual man or woman on his or her own merits, however, will undoubtedly reveal numerous instances where a particular person has some traits that defy these classifications.

Any time the distribution of a trait (physiological or behavioral) between the genders is statistically measured, one gender will have a predominant representation. And in some cases, the distribution will certainly be so heavily weighted toward one gender over the other as to become a *typically* masculine or *typically* feminine trait. But this should not be grounds to label such traits as *definitively* masculine or feminine, so that a person's brain gender is defined by these traits in opposition to their sexual gender.

The diagram below (while admittedly simplistic) represents the impact this new attitude about "brain gender" has on sexual orientation issues. Because modern society identifies homosexuality based on "the simultaneous incidence of same-sex eroticism *and gender role non-conformity*,"[31] males with a noticeable number of gender non-typical traits are not only being told that they have a "female" brain, but they are being encouraged to regard these traits as possible signs of a "homosexual orientation" as well.

Nowhere in Scripture are men or women exhorted to question their

[30] John Gray, *Men Are from Mars, Women Are from Venus: The Classic Guide to Understanding the Opposite Sex* (New York: HarperCollins, 2004), 3–4.

[31] "Homosexuality," *GLBTQ Encyclopedia: Social Sciences* (www.glbtq.com/social-sciences/homosexuality.html; accessed 12/28/2009). Italics added.

TABLE I

A Person's Traits	Same-sex sexual desires	Gender non-typical traits	Gender typical traits
Modern designations	"Homosexual"		"Straight"
Confessional designations	"Unnatural Affections"	"Natural Affections"	

gender identity based on tastes and mannerisms—let alone their sexual orientation. A noteworthy biblical example that warns against being over-dogmatic about identifying certain traits with certain genders is provided by the brothers, Jacob and Esau. While Esau was favored by his father and had many "man's man" characteristics and skills, Jacob evidently identified better with his mother and, we are told, was more domestic in his leanings: "When the boys grew up, Esau was a skillful hunter, a man of the field, while Jacob was a peaceful man, remaining at the tents. Isaac loved Esau because of his hunting stories,[32] but Rebekah loved Jacob" (Gen. 25:27–28). Physically, even, there were remarkable differences between Jacob and Esau. While the latter was hairy, Jacob was smooth skinned (25:11).

Notwithstanding Jacob's smooth and domestic traits, Scripture never so much as hints of any reason to regard Jacob as in anyway "not conforming" to his gender. And it does not appear that Jacob struggled with same-sex attractions either: his eyes were drawn to Rachel's beauty so that he loved her (Gen. 29:17–18), and he went on to father twelve sons and an undisclosed number of daughters by two wives and two concubines. Our purpose for citing the example of Jacob in this place is simply to note the fact that God does not intend for every man to be a "man's man" with the traits of an Esau. We might wonder how Jacob would be counseled if he were attending a public school,

---

[32] Most English translations render the Hebrew בְּפִיו כִּי־צַיִד (lit., "for game/hunting was in his mouth") in a way that implies it was Esau's food that had won Isaac's favoritism. This is possible, however, it is likely that this idiom refers to the hunting stories that filled Esau's mouth, rather than the game that filled Isaac's mouth. In either case, the translation of this detail is not consequential to the argument of the present paper.

today, and his tendency to avoid the rough-housing boys on the playground was noticed by a teacher trained in the modern ideas about "brain gender."

Melissa Hines (professor of Psychology at City University, London) begins her book on *Brain Gender* by stating, "*a characteristic that shows a sex difference is one that differs on the average for males and female of a given species.* Thus, a human characteristic is considered to show a sex difference if it differs for a group of boys or men in comparison to a group of girls or women."[33] In other words, as we have noted above, those traits which are generally found in one gender rather than another are considered a distinctive mark of that gender. This seems sensible enough; however, Dr. Hines' book is about identifying boys who have a female brain-gender and vice versa. While there may, indeed, be brain features which psychologists like Dr. Hines can associate with certain "more commonly male" and "more commonly female" traits, these do not justify calling a boy's brain "female" or a girl's brain "male." We believe it to be unbiblical (and unhelpful) to use such observations about *tendencies* of a given gender to *dogmatically impose* upon a person the burden of gender identities, which are the constructs of psychologists and contradictory to the two genders which God created us to uphold. Men like Jacob and men like Esau have very different personality traits, but biblically they are both equally and thoroughly male.

The church needs to be aware of these trends in our society, multiplying gender categories through the separation of sexuality and brain gender from one's physical gender. In particular, realizing that gender-typical traits are now being used to prescribe (rather than describe) gender identities, it becomes increasingly important that the church be careful not to fall into the trap of treating "sensitive men" as less masculine or "strong women" as not feminine and thereby contributing to a sense of gender confusion and the resulting burden of individuals being given one of society's new gender identities. While Scripture does prescribe the sexual orientation of each gender, Scripture does not prescribe the personality traits which belong to each gender. Furthermore, Christians in the church today often (following the world around us) describe certain personality characteristics as being "homosexual," as captured in the casual expression, "That's so gay!" When Christians adopt such stereotypes from the world, even when only used in casual conversation, it can be very

---

[33] Melissa Hines, *Brain Gender* (New York: Oxford University Press, 2004), 3–4 (italics original).

damaging. Such speech can cause men or women to believe that they are objectively "homosexual," especially if they have ever faced a same-sex temptation. Rather, they should be affirmed as being wholly masculine, or wholly feminine, exercising all the particular gifts and personality traits God has given them. In light of the widespread gender confusion of our age, the church needs to be Reformed even in our casual speech if we are to think and speak rightly about sexuality and personality.

IV

Hermeneutical Issues of the Homosexuality Debate

The church's interpretation of biblical texts on same-sex issues seemed clear and straightforward for centuries. It is only with the new perspectives on sexuality emerging in the last century that a vigorous re-examination of these texts has begun. Such re-examination of the church's exegesis can be a healthy exercise of our *semper reformanda* heritage. However, we note several problematic hermeneutical presuppositions that seem to be decisive to the new interpretations which countenance same-sex "orientations" (and even same-sex practices). It is worth noting these presuppositional issues before engaging with the biblical texts themselves.

First of all, some biblical scholars have presupposed that, since same-sex *orientation (homosexuality)* is a modern discovery, and the biblical texts were written addressing same-sex *activity*, the various Scriptures really do not apply to homosexuality as we now understand it. For example, Victor Paul Furnish (professor of New Testament at Southern Methodist University) begins his essay on "The Bible and Homosexuality" by stating, "The question 'What does the Bible say about homosexuality?' is misleading in several ways… It fails to take into account the fact that the ancient world had no word or concept of 'homosexuality.'"[34] Of course, Professor Furnish is not ignorant

---

[34] Victor Paul Furnish, "The Bible and Homosexuality: Reading the Texts in Context," 18; in, *Homosexuality in the Church* (Jeffrey S. Siker, ed.), 18–35.

of the widespread, same-sex behaviors of ancient societies. However, as he summarily concludes toward the end of his essay, "There is nothing in the Bible about homosexuality understood as a 'condition,' since the ancient world had no conception of anything like sexual orientation."[35]

While it is certainly true that Scripture does not speak of same-sex issues within the categories created by modern psychology, we deny the assumption that men like Professor Furnish infer from this fact: namely, that the biblical writings addressing same-sex *activities* were not also intended to address those inner dispositions which the modern terminology define as an "orientation."[36]

In his own exegesis of various Old Testament laws in the Sermon on the Mount, Jesus teaches us an important lesson about how the activity-(rather than psychology-) focused texts of Scripture are to be interpreted. He taught, for example: "You have heard that it was said to those of old, 'You shall not murder; and whoever murders will be liable to judgment.' But I say to you that everyone who is angry with his brother will be liable to judgment..." (Matt. 5:21–22) Murder is an activity, but Jesus teaches us that, when Scripture addresses this activity, we are to understand that the vast and complex array of underlying dispositions (in this case, anger is the one he identifies) are also being addressed. We are not suggesting that a person's inner struggle with anger, which may or may not result in activities like striking or murder, is comparable to an inner struggle with same-sex attraction. All we want to point out from this example of Jesus' own exegesis is that texts which address activities *are intended* to infer a concern for the underlying, psychological issues related to that activity as well, however complex they may be.

In fact, it is a general feature of ancient languages like Hebrew that concepts and dispositions were typically talked about by referring to their concrete expressions. But, as Jesus' Sermon on the Mount illustrates, the influence of Greek ways of discourse throughout the world leading up to the New Testament period had introduced a need to be more explicit about the abstract issues behind action-focused texts like "you shall not murder." The New Testament writers therefore, while continuing to employ many Hebraic ways of speaking, also show an increased tendency to address abstract ideas.

---

[35] Victor Paul Furnish, "The Bible and Homosexuality," 30.

[36] Cf., Greg L. Bahnsen, *Homosexuality: A Biblical View,* 66–69.

Thus, in the Sermon on the Mount, Jesus exegetes the concrete language of various Old Testament laws to show his Hellenized audience the guidance intended by these passages for inner tendencies, as well as external activities.

Getting more directly to the subject at hand, we also find the Apostle Paul in Romans 1 instructing his audience in Hellenistic Rome on the brokenness of mankind's sexual "nature" (φύσις) indicated by same-sex activities, and the "dishonorable passions" (πάθη ἀτιμίας) and "inner yearnings" (ὄρεξις) behind the same (Rom. 1:26–27). Thus, while it is true that neither the Old Testament nor the New Testament writers discussed *homosexuality* in quite the same manner as it is defined by modern psychology, this does not mean the biblical writers were ignorant of, nor failing to address, the internal dispositions of men and women with same-sex desires.

Actually, as Robert Gagnon points out, there is a fair bit of evidence that some philosophers and teachers in the ancient world were keenly aware of desires so deep as to warrant characterization as an innate orientation.[37] For example, Plato famously satired the sexual practices of his fellow Greeks, with a creation myth depicting the creation of humanity in three types: a conjoined man-woman being, a conjoined man-man being, and a conjoined woman-woman being; and that an offended Zeus cut these beings in two, leaving some men perpetually longing to be rejoined to their female counterpart, while others long to be rejoined to their same-sex counterpart.[38] Plato's myth for the origin of sexual dispositions represents an ancient perception of sexual identity on some level akin to an "inner orientation." Likewise, Aristotle believed that some men who are sexually attracted to other men are so disposed "by nature," while others are so inclined "from habit" (that is, from some stimulating event).[39] We cite these examples simply to demonstrate that

---

[37] Robert A. J. Gagnon, *The Bible and Homosexual Practice*, 384–5.

[38] Plato, *Symposium*, 189C–193D. Notably, a 5th century A.D. rabbinic commentary on Genesis borrowed Plato's idea and gives a similar interpretation of Gen. 1:26, "When the Holy Blessed One created *adam*, God created him/it *androgynous*, for it is said, *Male and female created He them*... When the Holy Blessed One created *adam*, God created it two-faced, then God split it and made it of two backs..." (*Genesis Rabbah* 8:1). Translation from, Gwynn Kessler, "Bodies in Motion: Preliminary Notes on Queer Theory and Rabbinic Literature," 402–5; in *Mapping Gender in Ancient Religious Discourses* (Todd Penner and Caroline Vander Stichele, eds., BIS 84; Leiden: Brill, 2007), 389–409.

[39] Aristotle, *Nicomachean Ethics*, 1148b, 28–34. Note, however, that Aristotle regarded the natural disposition toward same-sex desire as being a disorder "contrary to nature."

even ancient thinkers (writing long before the 19th century social reformers coined their terms) were not naïve concerning the kinds of inner, identity-level issues behind many same-sex behaviors. With such sensitivity to the depth of these feelings among non-biblical writers of the ancient world, we certainly ought not make the mistake of supposing that the inspired prophets and apostles were naïve concerning the intensity of same-sex thoughts and feelings behind same-sex activities.

For such reasons as these, we cannot accept the presupposition that Scripture's primary focus on same-sex *activity* means that the biblical texts are irrelevant to modern questions about same-sex *orientation*.

Secondly, many of the new interpretations are built upon the view that Scripture is an evolving collection of religious understandings, with different generations of ancient believers modifying the faith (and redacting the texts) from earlier generations. For instance, Dan O. Via posits the following basis for his handling of the Bible's texts on same-sex issues:

> In the Bible itself the revelation of God's Word occurs when some person or community within Israel or the church reinterprets past tradition in order to give it new meaning in the present. Revelation occurs as the reinterpretation of tradition. This is how, for example, the Gospels got written. If the revelation of God is not to remain fixed in the past, the reinterpretive process that produced the Bible must continue in the life of the Christian community.[40]

> Based on this presupposition concerning the nature of Scripture, Dr. Via is able to acknowledge that various biblical passages do, in their original setting, regard "homosexuality as sin,"[41] but nonetheless conclude today that, "Sexual desire is a part of being human, and in marriage each partner has an obligation to meet the sexual needs of the other. On what grounds should this legitimation of sexual practice be extended to gay and lesbian relationships? This is where rational scientific knowledge comes in. Recall that the Bible justifies in principle a critical use of scientific knowledge in theological-ethical discourse."[42]

---

[40] Dan O. Via, "The Bible, the Church, and Homosexuality," 38–39.

[41] Ibid. p. 10.

[42] Ibid. p. 32.

We are not persuaded that this presupposition is accurate (that Scripture is the product of men who revise the traditions of previous generations), thereby justifying the same approach to Scripture today. We understand that it is common in certain academic circles to view Scripture that way; however, we do not believe that presupposition has been demonstrated. Therefore, we cannot accept the approach to these passages that regards their opposition to same-sex behavior as somehow superseded by the New Testament's ethic of love informed by modern scientific insights into the purported biological origins of same-sex tendencies.

A third, problematic presupposition, which is sometimes employed when handling these texts, is a so-called "christocentric" interpretation. We certainly are zealous for Christ-centered interpretation, but the kind of "christocentric" hermeneutic often advanced in these debates is not consistent with an orthodox view of Scripture. This new form of "christocentric" interpretation often points to Barthian neo-orthodoxy for legitimization. We do not think it necessary, in this place, to examine the teachings of Karl Barth and whether his positions really do lead, necessarily, to the "christocentric" re-interpretations of Scripture embraced by those seeking to legitimize homosexuality in the church. But we are persuaded that Christ himself did not call the church to use his example to somehow "trump" the written Word. As we understand the example and teachings of Jesus, Christ saw himself as conforming to and fulfilling what was written, not providing an example to change or "re-interpret" past Scriptures.

Jack Rogers is an example of this new, "christocentric" hermeneutic. "Neo-orthodoxy's defining insight…," he writes, "was that people and God are known by personal encounter, not by rational analysis. The revelation of God comes *not* in an inspired book, but in the person of Jesus Christ, who is God incarnate."[43] Therefore, every passage of Scripture must be interpreted "through the lens of Jesus' redemptive life and ministry,"[44] which, as Rogers makes clear, means that the goal of "reconciliation" between different people groups is the "lens" through which Scripture must be read: "God's reconciling work in Jesus Christ [is] the heart of the gospel in any age and…the church…[is] especially

---

[43] Jack Rogers, *Jesus, the Bible, and Homosexuality: Explode the Myths, Heal the Church* (Louisville: Westminster John Knox, 2009), 37–38.

[44] Ibid. 39–40.

called to the ministry of reconciliation [i.e., between social groups]."[45] In Rogers' view, it was this "lens" of reconciliation that led his own denomination (the PCUSA) to move beyond racial discrimination, discrimination against women, and hard line views on divorce and remarriage.[46] He also believes that such a "shift[ing] from legalistic proof-texting to looking at Scripture through the lens of Jesus' life and ministry" will lead to an acceptance of gay marriages by the church: "Jesus did not set forth immutable laws to break people. Rather, he set forth an ideal toward which we all should strive—lifelong faithfulness in married relationships. That ideal could apply to gay and lesbian couples as well as to heterosexual couples."[47] Rogers' handling of the Leviticus laws against same-sex intercourse are illustrative, where, after identifying those prohibitions as matters of culturally conditioned ritual uncleanness (rather than moral violations),[48] he writes, "Jesus was concerned with purity of heart... When we see Jesus as the fulfillment of the law (Matt. 5:17), we understand that our challenge is not meticulously to maintain culturally conditioned laws, but rather, with Jesus, to love God and love our neighbor (Matt. 22:36–40) [which Rogers understands to mean affirming homosexuality]."[49]

There is much kindness and graciousness in Dr. Rogers' expressions which is commendable. We simply disagree with this presupposition that the "christocentric lens" removes the calling of God to seek transformation of sexual brokenness as a vital (and powerful!) part of Christ's work of reconciliation. We fully concur with the urgent pleas of such exegetes as Rogers for greater compassion (and less fear and prejudice) toward those who experience same-sex attractions. However, this kind of presupposition that Christ's ministry is one of acceptance toward, it would seem, all lifestyles shapes the results of exegesis before one even begins. The question that needs to be determined

---

[45]Ibid. 46–47. Cf., the PCUSA's *Confession of 1967* which Rogers quotes as embodying this hermeneutical approach for that branch of the church.

[46] Jack Rogers, *Jesus, the Bible, and Homosexuality*, 40–44.

[47]Ibid. 44.

[48] That תּוֹעֵבָה ("abomination") refers not only to ritual uncleanness, as asserted by Rogers, but can describe ethical and other wrongs as well, is seen, e.g., in Deut. 25:13–16; Prov. 6:16–19; 8:7; Amos 5:10; Mic. 3:9. (See, Michael A. Grisanti, תעב [#9493], *New International Dictionary of Old Testament Theology and Exegesis* [Willem A. VanGemeren, ed.; Carlisle, UK: Paternoster Press, 1996], 4.314–18.)

[49] Jack Rogers, *Jesus, the Bible, and Homosexuality*, 69.

from the Scripture is whether, in fact, christocentric reconciliation with those with same-sex desires involves a *transformation* of their "sexual identity" or a *legitimization* of it.

Such hermeneutical presuppositions—that biblical texts on same-sex acts do not apply to homosexual identity; that the Bible is an evolving document; or that all Scripture should be read through a lens of "social reconciliation"— are not consistent, in our view, with the orthodox reverence for Scripture stated in the *Westminster Confession of Faith:*

> Although the light of nature and the works of creation and providence do so far manifest the goodness, wisdom, and power of God, as to leave men unexcusable; yet are they not sufficient to give that knowledge of God and of His will, which is necessary unto salvation. Therefore it pleased the Lord, at sundry times, and in divers manners, to reveal Himself, and to declare that [revelation] His will unto His Church; and afterwards, for the better preserving and propagating of the truth, and for the more sure establishment and comfort of the Church against the corruption of the flesh, and the malice of Satan and of the world, to commit the same wholly unto writing; which maketh the Holy Scripture to be most necessary....
>
> The Old Testament in Hebrew...and the New Testament in Greek..., being immediately inspired by God..., are therefore authentical; so as, in all controversies of religion, the Church is finally to appeal unto them... The infallible rule of interpretation of Scripture is the Scripture itself: and therefore, when there is a question about the true and full sense of any Scripture (which is not manifold, but one) it must be searched and known by other places that speak more clearly. (*WCF* 1:1, 8–9).

We would urge ministers and laymen to be alert for these kinds of hermeneutical errors when encountering those who quote Scripture to contradict the historic stance of the church on same-sex issues.

V

Exegesis and Confessional Statements

While the whole of Scripture must be considered in this discussion, scholars regularly focus on certain passages that explicitly address same-sex issues. In this section of this paper, we will succinctly state the positions of representative "progressive" scholars on each of these texts, along with what we believe to be a proper interpretation of these passages as they relate to the homosexuality debate. While the exegesis of biblical texts is our only authority, confessional statements offer us the fruits of the church's exegesis in ages past. We will, therefore, also consider what the Westminster Standards say to us about same-sex issues.

We recognize that there is a broad range of views with respect to each of these passages, and we are not going to try to be comprehensive in this paper. When stating the position of contrary scholars, we are stating the views of those who wish to take Scripture seriously, thus we are not interacting with those who discount its validity altogether.

Finally, by way of preliminary remarks on this section, we want to acknowledge our particular dependence on a number of commentaries and exegetical treatments of these passages. Rather than providing footnotes to reflect our extensive reliance on others all through the following exegesis, we want to acknowledge, up front, our dependence on various standard commentaries along with conversations with various experts in the field, and the following key works: Greg L. Bahnsen, *Homosexuality: A Biblical Perspective;*

Robert A. J. Gagnon, *The Bible and Homosexual Practice: Texts and Hermeneutics.* Key sources for "progressive" interpretations of these passages include: Dan O. Via, "The Bible, the Church, and Homosexuality;" Jack Rogers, *Jesus, the Bible, and Homosexuality: Explode the Myths, Heal the Church.*

1. Genesis 1:27–28; 2:20–25—The Creation of Man

These passages in Genesis—as the foundational statement of God's design for human gender and sexual orientation—lay the groundwork for all that subsequent Scripture has to say about marriage and sexuality. Thus, it is imperative to pay attention to the creation account's introduction of gender and sexual orientation before treating those texts which deal specifically with same-sex questions.

Genesis 1:27 states that God "created man in his own image…male and female he created them." The church has traditionally (and we believe, rightly) understood this to mean that God created mankind in two distinct genders: male and female. These are not two poles on a continuum—with some people having 100% male brains, some having 70% male/30% female brains, and, so on, across to 100% female brains.[50] Modern gender theory portrays gender as a continuum between two poles. However, Genesis clearly intends for us to understand male and female as two distinct categories of humanity (not poles on a continuum).

This is particularly evident in the appointment God makes of the man and woman to distinct roles in their relationship as husband and wife. We understand that traditional roles of men and women in marriage are also controversial, today. We will not take up that subject at length in this place,[51] but we do want to note that the church has historically understood Genesis 1–2 as teaching the social as well as the sexual roles prescribed for the sexes. As delicate as these issues have become in modern discourse, the historic interpretation remains the most sound exegetically.

According to Genesis, the woman was presented to the man by God (it was not the man who was presented to the woman); and then the man named the woman (it was not the woman who named the man); and the woman is said to be "a helper fit for him" (Gen. 2:20–23). Paul tells us in 1 Corinthians

---

[50] Cf., the discussion of gender, biological sex, and sexual orientation continua in Chapter III.

[51] For a fuller discussion of the roles of men and women in marriage, we recommend: John Piper and Wayne Grudem, eds., *Recovering Biblical Manhood and Womanhood: A Response to Evangelical Feminism* (Wheaton, Ill.: Crossway, 2006).

11:8–10 and Ephesians 5:22–32 that this example is a lesson on the *two*, gender-consistent roles in a marriage. The woman is called to honor and support the husband, and the husband is called to lead, love, and care for the wife. There may be many personality differences which vary the way different couples work out this relationship, and some women may be more decisive by nature than their husbands and husbands may, at times, be more emotional by nature than their wives. Nevertheless, biblically, there are two roles within the marriage and the man is always appointed to the role of headship (meaning responsibility, not implying superiority) with the woman in a role of honored support (cf., *WCF* 4.2; *Reformed Presbyterian Testimony* [*RPT*] 4.6). There is not a continuum of marital roles taught in Genesis 2; but two roles which are assigned by gender—and a person's gender, biblically understood, is the same thing as his/her biological sex.

It is in the same context that Genesis also describes the sexual orientation of the man and woman for one another in the same, two, distinct categories: "Therefore a man shall leave his father and his mother and hold fast to his wife, and they shall become one flesh" (Gen. 2:24). There is certainly more intended in that expression than sexual intimacy; nevertheless, these references to physical bonding ("holding fast" and becoming "one flesh") certainly include sexual intimacy.[52] Jesus quotes this creation example as the basis for the institution of marriage and for restricting sexual relations to marriage (Matt. 19:4–12). But the pattern also shows us the two distinct categories assigned to marry and engage in sexual communion: a man and a woman. Just as later biblical writers saw two, distinct marital roles in this passage (not a continuum of marital roles); so, later biblical writers show us that these are two, distinct, gender-specific *sexual* roles in marriage as well. As Paul teaches the Corinthians, "…each man should have his own wife and each woman her own husband" (1 Cor. 7:2). Furthermore, in a discussion about adultery, Jesus pointed to this passage as setting the prescriptive pattern for restricting all sexual relations to the marriage of, specifically, a male and a female: "From the beginning of creation, 'God made them male and female. Therefore a man shall leave his father and mother and

---

[52] "'One flesh' does not refer to sexual intimacy in a narrow way, but recognizes that man and woman constitute an indissoluble unit of humankind from *every* perspective. Hence the author refers to but does not focus on the sexual relationship…" (Terence E. Fretheim, "Genesis," 354; in Leander E. Keck, *et al*, eds., *New Interpreter's Bible: Volume I* [Nashville: Abingdon, 1994], 319–674.)

hold fast to his wife, and they shall become one flesh'..." (Mk. 10:6–8). It is not simply the monogamy and fidelity of Genesis 2, abstractly, which Scripture sets before us as prescriptive. It is also the exclusively "heterosexual orientation" of that marriage which is prescriptive in Genesis 2.[53]

To sum this up: Genesis 1 and 2 shows us, not a "continuum" of family leadership positions marked out by the creation of the man and the woman, but two distinct roles *socially* oriented to one another (i.e., head and helper). This *social orientation* is determined by anatomical gender (not personality traits). Likewise, there is not a "continuum" of sexuality introduced in the creation account, but two distinct roles *sexually* oriented for one another. This orientation, also, is shown to be determined by the anatomical gender of the individual.

To evade the force of this passage, some commentators insist (to quote Victor Paul Furnish as an example) that "this is an 'aetiological' account, told in order to explain why things *are* as they are, not to prescribe what people *ought* to do... The[se texts] are not about God's will for individual members of the species [e.g., that a man should only have sex with a woman, and that only in marriage] but only about what is typical of the species as a whole [e.g., that mankind is a sexual being]."[54] But Professor Furnish ignores the fact that Paul, Jesus, and other biblical voices repeatedly point back to this very set of passages as *prescriptive* for the social *and* sexual roles of the two genders which God designed.

Man's sexual identity and function were determined by God at creation, and thus any contrary desire, including homosexual desire, can only be rightly explained as a consequence of Adam's fall in sin. As Christians, we follow a Savior who makes all things new as he re-creates a new humanity (Rev. 21:5). Christ redeems and restores men and women to be what God intended. Thus, the redeemed will only find true hope, joy, and restoration by delighting in what God, at creation, has declared to be "very good" (Gen. 1:31).

2. *Genesis 19:1–29 — Sodom and Gomorrah*

The Sodom and Gomorrah account in Genesis 19 is traditionally understood to illustrate God's judgment on same-sex sins. Those seeking biblical affirmation for homosexuality suggest that the real sin of Sodom was their pride, laziness, and lack of care for the poor and needy, not same-sex

---

[53] Cf., pp. 14–15.

[54] Victor Paul Furnish, "The Bible and Homosexuality," 21, 23.

activity. They often quote Ezekiel 16:49–50, where Ezekiel rehearses Sodom's sins in the following words: "Look, this was the iniquity of your sister Sodom: She and her daughter had pride, fullness of food, and abundance of idleness; neither did she strengthen the hand of the poor and needy. And they were haughty and committed abomination before me; therefore I took them away as I saw fit." Based on this commentary on Sodom's sins in Ezekiel, it is said that Genesis 19 merely recounts that the men of the city attempted to gang rape Lot's guests (and gang rape is evil when committed by "heterosexuals," too). Thus, some scholars suggest that Genesis 19 has nothing to contribute to the modern discussion regarding *consensual* homosexual relationships.

We agree that Sodom was condemned for many sins as Ezekiel makes explicit, and became a prototype in Scripture for a sinful culture. Same-sex behavior was not the only sin of Sodom, and it is wrong to interpret the story as being only or even mostly about judgment on homosexuality. However, the longing of the men of Sodom to "know" Lot's guests is prominently displayed as one clear example of their sinfulness, so its characterization of same-sex lust as part of Sodom's sin cannot be too hastily dismissed. In that account, Lot himself calls their same-sex lust sinful when he urges them to not "do so wickedly," and instead offered his daughters to the men. Lot regarded the same-sex character of this attack as particularly sinful, not just the fact that it was violent.

When Ezekiel gives his list of sins for which Sodom was condemned, he was not giving an exhaustive list. This is seen in the fact that Ezekiel ends his list of specific injustices with a final, generic phrase, "and [they] committed abomination before me" (v. 50). Ezekiel specifically tells us that the economic injustices mentioned are not the whole story; other abominations were also being committed. The reason Ezekiel only specified the economic sins of Sodom was because those were the sins that also characterized Judah in his own day. After all, Ezekiel was really preaching against Judah (not Sodom), so he only mentioned the sins of Sodom that were also present in Judah in his own day. Perhaps Judah was not guilty of same-sex sins, so that leaving that sin unspecified better served Ezekiel's purpose. In fact, since sexual sins are a prominent feature of the Sodom account, it may be that the reason the people of Judah thought they were better than Sodom and safe from the same demise was because they were not guilty of those prominent sins which they knew were behind Sodom's condemnation. We cannot know for certain why Judah thought they were not deserving of the same judgment as they knew Sodom suffered. But what we do know is that Ezekiel sought to point out to Judah that there were actually many sins in Sodom of which they also were guilty. In other words, the absence of any specific mention of same-sex lust in Ezekiel's list does not negate the presence of those sins in Sodom, especially since Genesis 19 frankly tells us such sins were part of the city's condemnation. Ezekiel's word choices simply let us know that it was the economic injustices present in Sodom that were also present in Judah in Ezekiel's day.

Finally, Jude 7 confirms that the sexual immorality of the city was one of the reasons it was destroyed (even if Ezekiel does not explicitly mention any sexual sins in his list).[55] The only example of immorality in Sodom which Scripture gives to us is their same-sex advances on Lot's guests, so that it is most natural to understand Jude's reference as confirming that the same-sex lusts of the men of Sodom was regarded as sinful before God.

We readily accept that same-sex behavior was not the only sin of Sodom. Genesis reports that there were many sins (e.g., economic sins, and so forth) in Sodom and Gomorrah, "the outcry of which" reached to heaven (18:20). The reason the two angels were sent was to search out whether there were grounds for mercy, or if the cities truly were deserving of judgment (18:21–33). That Genesis puts forward the same-sex lust of the inhabitants as the representative affront which the two angels encountered on their judicial examination of the cities' guilt, and based on which Sodom's fate was sealed, should not be minimized by observations of other sins that were also widespread in Sodom. Same-sex lust was not the only sin of Sodom and the surrounding towns, but we cannot accept as biblically sound those interpretations that minimize the importance of same-sex lust as part of—and, indeed, representative of—Sodom's sins.

3. Judges 19:1–30—The Levite's Concubine

The story of the Levite's concubine in Judges 19 has many similarities to the account of Sodom, so that many of the comments made above apply here, as well. As with regard to the Sodom account, some modern interpreters argue that the real sin in Judges 19 was in the desire for rape, not the fact that it was a *same-sex* rape attempt. We grant that rape (whether "heterosexual" or "homosexual") is condemned by this passage. However, it seems that the

---

[55] See the further exegesis of Jude 7, on p. 48–50.

fact that the rape here attempted was specifically same-sex rape is intended to illustrate just how deeply confused Israel had become by this time in history. In other words, this text seems designed to convey the sense of a society where (to borrow a characterization from Jude 15) "ungodly deeds" are being committed in "an ungodly manner."

4. Leviticus 18:22 and 20:13 — The Mosaic Prohibitions

Leviticus 18:22 reads, "You shall not lie with a male as with a woman. It is an abomination (תּוֹעֵבָה)." Similarly, Leviticus 20:13 states, "If a man lies with a male as he lies with a woman, both of them have committed an abomination (תּוֹעֵבָה). They shall surely be put to death. Their blood shall be upon them."

"Progressive" scholars generally understand these passages in one of two ways. One view understands that these passages condemn homosexual activity only as it was being practiced in a particular way in the land Israel was about to settle. Male prostitution was sometimes connected with fertility cults in the ancient world, and (it is said) it was really participation in such sexual, fertility cults that was being forbidden in these passages. Thus, some scholars hold that this passage does not condemn *all* same-sex behavior, but merely that which is illicit, destructive, and idolatrous.

A second view understands these prohibitions in Leviticus to be ceremonial (not moral) laws. That is, such commands were given, not because same-sex activity was immoral, but because same-sex activity (like "heterosexual" activity) left a person ceremonially unclean. This view equates the "abomination" of same-sex behavior with the "abomination" of sexual emissions (Lev. 15:16–30) or menstruation (Lev. 15:19),[56] which no longer make a person unclean since the ceremonial laws are fulfilled in Christ.

It is true that the Hebrew word for "abomination" (תּוֹעֵבָה) is sometimes used to refer to ritual uncleanness. However, this does not mean that the word refers only to matters of ritual uncleanness. There are at least seven reasons to understand that the Leviticus prohibitions of same-sex behavior is a moral injunction forbidding same-sex activity for all time:

---

[56] Some also draw a comparison to the "abomination" of unclean meats. For example, Leviticus 11:13 reads, "And these you shall regard as an abomination (שֶׁקֶץ) among the birds; they shall not be eaten, they are an abomination: the eagle, the vulture, the buzzard..." Note, however, that the Hebrew words for "abomination" here is not the same as used in the passages on same-sex "abominations."

In these verses, the word "male" (זָכָר) is used and not the word for "male-prostitute" (קָדֵשׁ; cf., Deut. 23:17–18). The most prominent expressions of same-sex behavior in the ancient world may, indeed, have been found in pagan worship, but Leviticus 18:22 and 20:13 forbid men in general (not just male temple-prostitutes) from lying with other men "as a man lies with a woman."

Leviticus identifies same-sex behavior as abnormal by contrasting it to the norm, "as a man lies with a woman." The creation order of a man joining himself to a woman as his wife (Gen. 2:23–24) is here being cited as normative.

Other forms of intercourse in this Leviticus passage that vary from the cited norm ("as a man lies with a woman")—such as bestiality, adultery, and incest—are recognized by the church as permanent prohibitions (not temporary, ceremonial laws). It seems this sin would be permanent, as well.

Since the other sexuality laws of Leviticus 18:1–30 and 20:1–21 (adultery, bestiality, and incest) were not limited to their practice in cultic settings, it is inconsistent to regard the prohibition of same-sex sex as only referring to ritual same-sex behavior.

Leviticus 20:13 prescribes capital punishment for both parties to the act, which contradicts the common argument that *consensual* same-sex relations are condoned by Scripture. In other words, this ban is not simply to prohibit abusive relationships, but consensual same-sex sex also.

The wider context of these passages, seen in Leviticus 18:24–30 and 20:22–24, teaches that these abominations are the reason for which the Canaanites were expelled from the land. These were not ceremonial laws only required of Israel, but moral laws required of all peoples. Leviticus 18:25 calls these activities "iniquity" (עָוֹן), not merely "uncleanness" (טָמֵא).

Finally, Deuteronomy 23:17–18 provides an example of an Old Testament law prohibiting same-sex cult prostitution. The fact that there is an Old Testament law which shows us what a focused condemnation of temple prostitution looks like strengthens the likelihood that the broader language used in Leviticus is indeed intended to address a much broader scope of same-sex activity than just temple prostitution.[57]

---

[57] In addition to the points listed, a possible New Testament allusion to these Leviticus passages also deserves note. In 1 Cor. 6:9, Paul forbids same-sex relations saying that "ἀρσενοκοῖται" (often translated "homosexuals") will not inherit the kingdom of God. The word ἀρσενοκοῖται is a compound formed by joining "male" (ἄρσην) and "bed" or "a place for lying" (κοίτη). It literally means, "man-bedders." This compound word

It is certainly correct that the Canaanite fertility cults (and the male-prostitution involved in those cults) are included in the purview of these Mosaic injunctions. But it overly narrows their intended scope to neglect their broader application. Greg Bahnsen notes that it would be improper to interpret the New Testament's general warnings against drunkenness as only referring to drunkenness at the Lord's Supper simply because other passages in the New Testament tell us that this was a particular problem in that time.[58] Similarly, it is improper to narrow the interpretation of these passages from Leviticus to understand them as referring only to fertility cult worship.[59]

5. 1 Corinthians 6:9–11—Paul's List of Defilements

First Corinthians 6:9–11 reads,

> Do you not know that the unrighteous will not inherit the kingdom of God? Do not be deceived. Neither fornicators, nor idolaters, nor adulterers, nor homosexuals, nor sodomites, nor thieves, nor covetous, nor drunkards, nor revilers, nor extortioners will inherit the kingdom of God. And such were some of you. But you were washed, but you were sanctified, but you were justified in the name of the Lord Jesus and by the Spirit of our God.

ἀρσενοκοῖται is not found in period Greek writings outside of Paul's epistle. However, Paul may have drawn these two words together from Lev. 18:22 and 20:13. In the Septuagint translation of both those verses, these same Greek words "man" and "bed" are used to describe the man who lies with a man. Many commentators believe Paul was alluding to this Old Testament law against "man-bedders" when he combined the same two words into the term used in his Corinthian statement on the same subject. If this is correct, it means that Paul's reference is a further indication that the Leviticus passages are not simply prohibiting temple prostitution or same-sex rape; Paul understood it as a prohibition against all same-sex sex.

[58] Greg L. Bahnsen, *Homosexuality: A Biblical View*, 45.

[59] As a further witness to this reading of Lev. 18:22 and 20:33, it is notable that the Qumran community cited these Leviticus laws in various lists of their community rules. Although the Qumran documents are neither inspired nor of any particular ecclesiastical authority, they provide a further witness that intertestamental Judaism saw these laws against "a man lying with a man as with a woman" as relevant even after the Canaanite cults with their male prostitutes were long gone. (See a list of these citations with brief discussion of them in William Loader, *The Dead Sea Scrolls on Sexuality: Attitudes Toward Sexuality in Sectarian and Related Literature at Qumran* [Grand Rapids: Eerdmans, 2009], 361.)

The focus of debate in this text revolves around the two Greek words here translated as "homosexuals" and "sodomites" at the end of verse nine. The first is the Greek word μαλακοὶ, which literally means "soft," or in moral contexts, "yielding." Thus, the word is sometimes translated "effeminate," and some interpreters believe Paul is simply condemning over-indulgence in luxury. It is true that the word can refer to "lovers of luxury" (loving soft clothes, dainty foods, etc.), but in period Greek the word was also used of the passive or penetrated partner, often the younger partner, in same-sex intercourse. It does not seem likely Paul is using the term to refer to the love of luxury, since enjoying dainty foods does not seem to be on the same par with the other sins here listed as excluding a person from God's kingdom. More importantly, the fact that this word μαλακοὶ is here paired with the Greek term ἀρσενοκοῖται confirms that Paul has the sexual meaning of the word in view.

While μαλακοὶ refers to the "effeminate" or receiving partner in same-sex intercourse, ἀρσενοκοῖται is a compound word formed by combining the words "male" (ἄρσην) and "bed" (κοίτη). The word literally means "a man-bedder," and it refers to the active or penetrating agent in same-sex intercourse. Paul uses both terms together in this passage to indicate the culpability of both partners in same-sex sins. (Note the parallel to Lev. 20:13 which makes the same point, and which Old Testament law Paul may actually be quoting from here; see, p. 44–45, footnote 57.) To limit these verses to prohibitions against male prostitution and indulgence in soft clothing does not, in our view, square with the natural reading of Paul's word choices. He is indeed identifying same-sex sex as among the serious sins out of which God is saving people.

It must be stressed before leaving this passage, that Paul is abundantly clear in this text that those involved in same-sex sex, like the fornicators, adulterers, and drunkards also listed here, can be redeemed. Paul testifies in this passage that there were some μαλακοὶ and ἀρσενοκοῖται who left that life behind and were now part of the Corinthian church. They had come to Christ and left behind their former identity as "homosexuals." They were no longer characterized by such terms—their identities had been changed. Paul boldly states that those who are still engaged in same-sex relationships should be labeled as such and called to repentance and a departure from that manner of life. But once such repentance takes place, the old manner of life *and* the old identity (for which Paul uses the aforementioned terms) are to be put away. It is also clear from Paul's writing, here, that these saints might still be tempted with the sins of their old way of life (that is the whole reason he is addressing these former vices in a letter to the saints in Corinth). Nevertheless, their identities had been forever changed in Jesus Christ such that they were not now to be known by those same-sex identities anymore than the sober man or the former thief would be known as a drunkard or thieves.

6. 1 Timothy 1:8-11—Paul's Applications of the Ten Commandments

In this passage, the Apostle gives another list of sins summarizing the Old Testament law, saying,

> But we know that the law is good if one uses it lawfully, knowing this: that the law is not made for a righteous person, but for the lawless and insubordinate, for the ungodly and for sinners, for the unholy and profane, for murderers of fathers and murderers of mothers, for manslayers, for fornicators, for sodomites (ἀρσενοκοίταις), for kidnappers, for liars, for perjurers, and if there is any other thing that is contrary to sound doctrine, according to the glorious gospel of the blessed God which was committed to my trust.

Some scholars relegate the term ἀρσενοκοίταις in this passage (the same term also used in 1 Cor. 6:9, and discussed earlier) to those who engage in sexual relations with male prostitutes (or perhaps to those who are abusive in same-sex relationships). However, Paul states that he is dealing with the law, and then gives examples roughly following the outline of the Ten Commandments, specifically from the fifth commandment to the ninth. The fact that Paul identifies the prohibition of ἀρσενοκοίταις as rooted in the seventh commandment along with reproach of fornication, and he does not introduce this as a violation of the first or second commandments, further demonstrates that idolatry (i.e., false worship through male temple prostitution) is not the primary force of this word in Paul's thought. By using the word-pair, πόρνοις and ἀρσενοκοίταις, to represent the seventh commandment, it seems that Paul is using period terms to condemn both "heterosexual" and "homosexual" lusts.[60]

---

[60] In fact, that Paul again uses the Greek term which he may have formed based on the

7. Jude 5–7—Sodom and Gomorrah, Remembered

Jude's short epistle includes a reference to the Sodom and Gomorrah story, in which he states, "But I want to remind you, though you once knew this, that the Lord, having saved the people out of the land of Egypt, afterward destroyed those who did not believe. And the angels who did not keep their proper domain, but left their own abode, He has reserved in everlasting chains under darkness for the judgment of the great day; as Sodom and Gomorrah, and the cities around them in a similar manner to these, having given themselves over to sexual immorality and gone after strange flesh (σαρκὸς ἑτέρας), are set forth as an example, suffering the vengeance of eternal fire" (Jude 5–7).

Jude uses an unusual expression to identify the nature of the immorality being condemned toward the end of this passage. The phrase σαρκὸς ἑτέρας literally means "strange flesh," which some interpreters take as a reference to the fact that the men of Sodom lusted after *angels* who visited Lot. Thus, their lust was after non-human flesh, which some interpreters take to be the proper force of this term. They reinforce this interpretation, then, by positing that the preceding reference to "the angels who did not keep their proper domain" is referring to the "sons of God" in Genesis 6:2 who "saw that the daughters of man were beautiful and took as their wives any they chose." Thus, it is argued, the two examples both refer to the atrocity of humans and angels engaging in sexual intercourse. Consequently, Jude's statement has nothing at all to do with same-sex relationships.

Obviously, this is a very complicated passage, and it is related to other complicated passages. A thorough treatment is not possible here. However, it is not generally held among reformed commentators that the best reading of Genesis 6 has in mind the idea of angels copulating with human women. Besides doubting that it is even possible for angels and women to bear offspring together (there were offspring from the unions in Genesis 6), most reformed commentators believe that Genesis 6 refers either to the godly line of Seth (called "sons of God") intermarrying with the ungodly line of Cain (called "sons of men"), or to the kings of the forming kingdoms of the early human race ("sons of mighty-ones," with *elohim* referring to human rulers not to God) taking many wives into their harems to secure their dynasties (i.e., the beginning of royal polygamy). The passage in Jude, then, cannot refer to Genesis 6, but instead must

---

Leviticus 18 and 20 passages may further indicate that Paul regarded those Leviticus texts as rooted in the seventh commandment, and therefore abiding moral laws, not ceremonial laws (cf., the discussion of 1 Cor. 6:9–11 on p. 45).

refer to the fall of the angels with Satan (there are numerous parallels between Jude and the account of Satan's fall in Isaiah 14). If this is correct, and Jude's reference to the sin of the angels refers to their rebellion, and not to intercourse with human women, then the sin of Sodom and Gomorrah in Jude should not be read as exactly conforming to the sin of the angels. We believe this is the correct understanding of the text: Jude 6 is recalling the rebellion of the angels in Isaiah 14; Jude 6 is not interpreting Gen. 6 as describing a sexual liaison between angels and human women.

Furthermore, Jude says that not only the men of Sodom lusted after "strange flesh," but he says that "Sodom and Gomorrah, and the surrounding cities" indulged in this sin. In Genesis 19, it was only Sodom that was visited by the angels. If Sodom and Gomorrah, and the other cities of the plain surrounding them, shared in the kind of sin which Jude has in mind, it must be the same-sex lust of the men of Sodom (rather than the unusual fact that, in that one incident, the men they were lusting after happened to be angels).[61]

Jude also uses the "sexual immorality" (ἐκπορνεύσασαι) and lust after "strange flesh" of these cities as a warning to his own audience. It is highly unlikely that he would be concerned about his own audience lusting after angel-flesh. Since Jude seems to expect that his audience be able to identify with Sodom and Gomorrah's sins, it seems "strange flesh" must refer to unnatural passions less exotic than angel-lust.

Finally, it should be noted that Jude's language places emphasis on the lust inside the men's hearts in a manner that seems to suggest that they knew what they were doing. The term for "having given themselves over to immorality" (ἐκπορνεύσασαι) is intensive and denotes extravagant lust. Further, the word for "gone after" (ἀπελθοῦσαι) amplifies the fact that they wholeheartedly gave themselves to their willful desires for "strange flesh." The men of Sodom did not know that the men behind Lot's doors were angels; their lust was for men. Jude's emphasis on the fact that the object of their lust was "strange flesh," and

---

[61] Jude actually says, "Sodom and Gomorrah, and the surrounding cities *likewise* ... pursued strange flesh." Some commentators understand the "likewise" to compare the sins of these cities with the sins of the angels in the previous verse. It may be, however, that the "likewise" is emphasizing the fact that the other cities of the plain followed Sodom and Gomorrah into the same sins and thus shared in their judgment, thus contributing to Jude's theme of warning his audience against following false teachers and sharing in their judgment. If this reading is correct, then the fact is emphatic: the cities of the plain all lusted *likewise* after "strange flesh," which means Jude cannot have angel-lust in view.

further that the men willfully pursued "strange flesh," adds to the sense that it was the same-sex nature of their longings (rather than the angelic nature of the objects of their longings) which Jude has in view.

While the phrase σαρκὸς ἑτέρας ("strange flesh") is an unusual expression for same-sex passions, it is not an unnatural way to describe same-sex desires. Simon Kistemaker explains, "The Greek reveals that in the case of duality (for example, male and female) the word *other* can mean 'a second of two' and in the context denote a difference of kind. Therefore, when the men of Sodom were interested in sexual relations with men, they perverted the created order of natural intercourse."[62] Yes, Jude uses an unusual phrase to describe same-sex intercourse and this whole passage is full of interpretative difficulties; however, we believe that the best interpretation is that Jude is indeed warning against sexual immorality in general and same-sex lusts in particular.

8. Romans 1:26–27—Paul on Unnatural Desire

In the opening chapter of Romans, Paul describes a long list of sins which characterize a society which is falling away from God. Included in that list is his statement that,

> For this reason God gave them up to vile passions. For even their women exchanged the natural use for what is against nature. Likewise also the men, leaving the natural use of the woman, burned in their lust for one another, men with men committing what is shameful, and receiving in themselves the penalty of their error which was due (Rom. 1:26–27).

Scholars defending biblical allowances for same-sex relationships have interpreted Romans 1:26-27 in a variety of ways. It has been suggested, for instance, that Paul was primarily concerned in this passage with elements tied to pagan worship: that he was confronting extreme and abusive forms of same-sex activity (perhaps even particular historical incidents); or that he was merely addressing the same-sex behavior he was familiar with which was "unnatural" (Paul simply was not personally acquainted with "homosexual Christians" who were same-sex oriented by nature and able to be as faithful and monogamous as are "heterosexual" Christian couples).

---

[62] Simon J. Kistemaker, *New Testament Commentary: James, Epistles of John, Peter and Jude* (Grand Rapids: Baker, 1996), 318.

Arguments suggesting that this text is only condemning certain kinds of abusive and cult-worship homosexual practices are based on a faulty understanding of Old Testament passages we have already considered. It is this last idea which is particularly concerning. It latches onto the phrase "against nature" in verse 27 and purports that Paul was concerned with perversion, not inversion. Dan O. Via states this position as follows: "Paul seems to have agreed with the generally held belief of the ancient world that there is only one sexual nature, what we would call a heterosexual nature. Therefore, what he is condemning as contrary to nature is homosexual acts by people with a heterosexual nature. His implied underlying principle is that if people choose to actualize their sexuality, their acts should be in accord with their nature or orientation. If Paul then could be confronted with the reality of homosexual orientation, consistency would require him to acknowledge the naturalness of homosexual acts for people with a homosexual orientation."[63] Other similar interpretations hold that Paul actually was aware that some "homosexuals by nature" were practicing in a manner consistent with their orientation, and he could have commended them; but, for the sake of brevity, he did not. In other words, these commentators hold that Romans 1:26–27 is condemning any individual engaging in sexual activity contrary to *his own, innate nature,* rather than condemning sexual activity that is contrary to the natural, created order.

This view fails to take into account the fact that the whole passage hearkens back to creation (vv. 20, 25), where God determined the nature of mankind's sexual make-up. He united a man and a woman as biblically natural partners. The point of Romans chapter one is that humanity has rebelliously twisted God's natural order, including the sexual design, hence God has given them over even further to the sin they crave. The point is not that individuals have different inborn identities with which they must act consistently (their *own* sexual nature), but that the Lord has established the normative identity of male and female for all humanity to be expressed sexually between only one man and one woman being joined as one flesh (*mankind's* sexual nature). Though some may indeed experience strong same-sex erotic attractions, God's people must know from Scripture that while such temptations are real and perhaps even biologically influenced, they are not objectively natural but the result of human sinfulness requiring redemption.

---

[63] Dan O. Via, "The Bible, the Church, and Homosexuality," 15.

9. Other texts

The previous texts are those which explicitly address same-sex issues, and thus are the one most prominently discussed in relation to questions about the Bible's teaching on "homosexuality." There are, however, two additional narratives that are sometimes deemed pertinent to the topic, and so will be briefly treated here, as well.

a. Ham's offense against Noah (Gen. 9:20–27)

This first of these is the account of Ham's offense against his father, Noah. The delicacy of the narrator has left unstated just how much Ham did in his violation of Noah during Noah's drunkenness. He simply writes, "Noah… became drunk and lay uncovered in his tent. And Ham, the father of Canaan, saw the nakedness of his father and told his two brothers outside" (Gen. 9:20–22). The passage obviously intends for us to recognize that it was a wrong within the general realm of same-sex violations, even if it was simply seeing and mocking his father's nakedness. In fact, by noting right away that this Ham was "the father of Canaan," and then later indicating that Noah placed a curse upon Ham's son Canaan, specifically, because of this sin, it is evident that the real focus of this text is on the same-sex indulgences of the Canaanites dwelling in the land in Moses' day, and for which they were being expelled from the land (see our earlier discussions of the sins of Canaan in relation to Lev. 18 and 20).

Once again, some interpreters tend to focus on *one* aspect of Ham's sin (the fact that his abuse of his father was incestuous in nature) to the exclusion of any other aspect of his sin being deemed wrong. However, it is common in narratives like these to show the horror of a people's sinfulness by piling layers of sin together, all of which have to be taken into account. In the sin of Sodom, as we earlier saw, a violation of hospitality *and* gang rape *and* same-sex lust are all being condemned. So here, the incestuous nature of Ham's offense is piled *on top* of the same-sex nature of his offense, *along* with the mocking or boasting nature of it, to create a full sense of grief at the presence of original sin even here amongst Noah's sons right after the flood.

b. David's love for Jonathan (2 Sam. 1:26)

It has often been claimed that David and Jonathan had a homosexual relationship and that the author merely suppressed references to erotic activity between the two men. Indeed Samuel did highlight a close relationship between the two (1 Sam. 18:1-5; 20:14-17, 41-42; 2 Sam. 1:26). However, these passages serve to demonstrate the loyalty of Jonathan to David as anointed heir to the throne, in spite of the fact that Jonathan was in line biologically to receive the throne instead of David. Never is there reference the men "knowing" one another or "lying" together. The point is that David was not a usurper of the throne but an advocate of Saul and his family, and that Jonathan wholeheartedly supported David's acquisition of the throne at this important transition in redemptive history. These two were not companions who destroyed one another, but they were friends who were closer than brothers.[64]

The fact that David's intimate friendship with another man has become subject to sexual suspicions illustrates one of the great tragedies of the modern effort to legitimize homosexuality. Al Mohler points out that close, same-sex friendships have been the ironic casualties of mainstreaming homosexuality. "Shakespeare and many other great authors spoke of nonsexual love between men in strongest terms," Mohler writes, "Similarly, when David is told of the death of his friend Jonathan, he cries, 'Your love to me was more wonderful than the love of women' (2 Samuel 1:26) ... What was once understood to be pure and undefiled is now subject to sniggering and disrespect."[65] It is the mainstreaming of homosexuality which has led to the presupposition of "more than meets the eye" in relationships like that of David and Jonathan.

10. Confessional Standards

The Westminster Standards say very little, explicitly, about the subject of same-sex attractions. The only direct reference is in the *Larger Catechism*, question 139 (dealing with the Seventh Commandment). The entire question is quoted here, with the relevant phrase and its proof texts highlighted:

Q. What are the sins forbidden in the seventh commandment?

---

[64] Note the thorough treatment of David and Jonathan's relationship by Markus Zehnder, "Observations on the Relationship between David and Jonathan and the Debate on Homosexuality," in *WTJ* 69 (2007), 127–74.

[65] R. Albert Mohler, Jr., Desire and Deceit: The Real Cost of the New Sexual Tolerance (Colorado Springs: Multnomah, 2008), 88. Mohler relies extensively, in this section of his book, on Anthony Esolen, "A Requiem for Friendship: Why Boys Will Not Be Boys and Other Consequences of the Sexual Revolution," *Touchstone* (Sept. 2005).

A. The sins forbidden in the seventh commandment, besides the neglect of the duties required, are adultery, fornication, rape, incest, *sodomy, and all unnatural lusts*; all unclean imaginations, thoughts, purposes, and affections; all corrupt or filthy communications, or listening thereunto; wanton looks, impudent or light behaviour, immodest apparel; prohibiting of lawful, and dispensing with unlawful marriages; allowing, tolerating, keeping of stews, and resorting to them; entangling vows of single life, undue delay of marriage; having more wives or husbands than one at the same time; unjust divorce, or desertion; idleness, gluttony, drunkenness, unchaste company, lascivious songs, books, pictures, dancings, stage plays; and all other provocations to, or acts of uncleanness, either in ourselves or others.

"Prov. 5:7; Heb. 13:4; Gal. 5:19; 2 Sam. 13:14; 1 Cor. 5:1; *Rom. 1:24, 27; Lev. 20:15, 16*; Matt. 5:28; Matt. 15:19; Col. 3:5; Eph. 5:3, 4; Prov. 7:5, 21, 22; Isa. 3:16; 2 Pet. 2:14; Prov. 7:10, 13; 1 Tim. 4:3; Lev. 18:1–21; Mal. 2:11,12; 1 Kings 15:12; 2 Kings 23:7; Deut. 23:17,18; Lev. 19:29; Jer. 5:7; Prov. 7:24–27; Matt. 19:10,11; 1 Cor. 7:7–9; Gen. 38:26; Mal. 2:14, 15; Matt. 19:5; Mal. 2:16; Matt. 5:32; 1 Cor. 7:12, 13; Ezek. 16:49; Prov. 23:30–33; Gen. 39:10; Eph. 5:4; Ezek. 23:14–16; Isa. 23:15-17; Isa. 3:16; Mark 6:22; Rom. 13:13; 1 Pet. 4:3; 2 Kings 9:30 with Jer. 4:30 and Ezek. 23:40."

Of course, the Westminster divines were not acquainted with the modern distinction between sexual activity and desires on the one hand, and sexual orientation on the other. Nevertheless, the decision to pair the terms "sodomy" (deeds) and "unnatural lusts" (desires) reflects an understanding on their part that both same-sex sex *and* same-sex desires are violations of the seventh commandment. While the divines did not have the claims of modern science before them to prompt any reference to same-sex *orientation* in their statement, they nonetheless clearly intend their statement to address the entire internal and external scope of human sexuality.[66] We offer the

---

[66] Cf., *WCF* 6.2, where the Westminster divines further state their understanding that original sin "defiled … all the faculties and parts of soul and body." The divines did not possess the insights of modern science into the ways in which a person's biology and other factors (i.e., "orientation") might contribute to a propensity to certain desires. Nevertheless, neither were they ignorant of the fact that sins are rooted in our fallen

following diagram to illustrate the overlap of categories represented by the 17th century terminology of the divines and the terminology of modern science:

TABLE II

Confessional Categories	Modern categories
External Sexuality (e.g., acts like "sodomy")	**External** Sexuality (e.g., acts like "same-sex sex")
Internal Sexuality (e.g., "unnatural lusts")	**Conscious internal** sexuality (e.g., "same-sex desires") **Subconscious internal** sexuality (e.g., "sexual orientation")
God's **natural order** (Gen. 1-2) male/female sexual compatibility	*(no universal, standard orientation is recognized)*

It is a modern convention to divide man's "inner sexuality" into distinct categories of conscious thought and subconscious orientations. To interpret the Catechism as addressing only *conscious* thought (to the *exclusion* of subconscious urgings) by its terminology is to force modern conventions upon the text, anachronistically. Rather, it should be understood that the intention of the Catechism statement is to address the *entire* inner and external life of the one whose sexuality is contrary to nature as God designed it.

While this statement in the *Larger Catechism* is the only explicit reference to same-sex issues in the Westminster Standards, the *Confession of Faith's* chapter on marriage is relevant when it stipulates that "Marriage [and, by inference, all the privileges of marriage, including sex] is to be between one man and one woman" (*WCF* 24.1).[67]

nature, which includes "all faculties and parts of soul and body."

[67] Cf., the *Testimony of the Reformed Presbyterian Church* 24.2: "Premarital sex relations or promiscuous sex practices as well as homosexuality and other perversions of the natural order are violations of God's law and purpose. All should strive to discipline their sexual desires, maintain purity of thought and practice, and avoid situations which lead to sexual temptation. (1 Cor. 6:9, 15–20; 1 Cor. 5:1–5, 9–11; 1 Cor. 7:8–9; Rom. 1:26–28; Phil. 4:8; Prov. 5)."

VI

Pastoral Implications

In the preceding pages, we have explored the issue of homosexuality from several angles. We have examined the subject from the perspectives of history, science, biblical interpretation, and Christian doctrine. But homosexuality is not just an issue to try to understand, it is a struggle experienced by real people. In this final (and perhaps most important) section, we want to offer guidance for pastors and counselors to minister God's grace to individuals wrestling with same-sex desires.

Sadly, those caught in the throes of same-sex temptations are often unwilling to seek help in the church. Even more tragically, Christians are often afraid to reach out and offer Christ's love to those identified as "homosexual." A blend of incomplete facts and inaccurate stereotypes on both sides have tended toward a fear of reaching out.[68] In the church, this uneasiness results in a tendency to speak much about the sin of homosexuality, but to offer little real help to those struggling with it. We hope the following material will be helpful for improving our ministry as Christ's church to men and women with same-sex tendencies.

1. Preliminary Considerations
A few preliminary points need to be made up front. First, while same-sex

---

[68] Illustrating the stereotype of the church fostered in the gay community: Louis Crompton, *Homosexuality and Civilization* (Cambridge, Mass.: First Harvard University Press, 2006).

sins are treated very seriously in Scripture, they are not all that different from other temptations common to human experience. Homosexual sins are not unforgivable, nor is homosexual temptation a hopeless plight. Christians must avoid the stereotype of homosexuality as a sin greater than all others,[69] along with the presumption that those experiencing same-sex desires necessarily chose to feel that way.[70]

Same-sex temptation is just one among the many different burdens carried by each of us who need the redeeming work of Christ in our lives. Like many other temptations, same-sex desires often arise without warning and feel hopelessly overpowering. But all human brokenness is within reach of the Gospel's power.

The Apostle Paul offers a powerful word of hope for overcoming all manner of sinful passions in his first epistle to the church in Corinth:

> [You once were] sexually immoral, … idolaters, … adulterers, … [those] who practice homosexuality, … thieves, … greedy, … drunkards, … revilers, … swindlers … Such were some of you. But you were washed, you were sanctified, you were justified in the name of the Lord Jesus Christ and by the Spirit of our God … God raised the Lord and will also raise us up by his power (1 Cor. 6:9–14).

Notice three things about this passage. First of all, note that homosexual sin is listed right alongside other, likewise grievous human temptations. Note also that each of the passions Paul lists here is a yearning that can be humanly uncontrollable in its bondage. But note also that all of these struggles are described as *former* identities from which the Corinthian believers were delivered by the power of Christ's resurrection. The Scripture gives us tremendous hope in the face of all kinds of deep-seated passions.

We do not possess within ourselves the power to overcome *any* sinful passion. None of us can transform an alcoholic ("drunkard," in Paul's list above). None of us can grant full release, in our timing, to one wrestling with gambling temptations (included in the term "greedy" in Paul's list). Neither

---

[69] According to *WLC* 150, "All transgressions of the law of God are not equally heinous; but some sins in themselves, and by reason of several aggravations, are more heinous in the sight of God than others." The subsequent question (*WLC* 151) offers guidance for discerning what those aggravations are that make some sins more heinous than others.

[70] See fuller discussion of this in Chapter II.

is it within our power to work out deliverance from homosexual temptations. However, the Spirit of God is in the business of redeeming men and women from all manner of ungodly passions. It is the fact of Christ's resurrection that shows us the kind of power God applies to the healing of our brokenness. And God has been pleased to minister such transformations, not only to men and women of ancient Corinth, but he continues to do so today.

It is not considered "politically correct," today, to acknowledge that changes in sexual orientation are possible.[71] Deep-seated desires are never resolved easily. They are certainly not resolved by mere will-power or "steps of treatment." We dare not promise quick solutions; but neither should we shy away from the full hope of the Gospel for total redemption by the working of God's Spirit. Recent, scientifically rigorous studies of "religiously mediated change in sexual orientation" offer contemporary confirmation that the God of Paul and the believers in Corinth truly is still redeeming men and women from all manner of humanly uncontrollable passions today.[72]

Christians must avoid the stereotype of homosexuality as worse than all other sins and beyond the reach of God's grace. Instead, we must replace that stereotype with robust Gospel hope.

Secondly, when ministering to a person with same-sex temptations, we should not treat this one area of struggle in his or her life as somehow isolated from others. Whenever we discuss a particular kind of sin in an abstract manner, we tend to talk about it in a vacuum—as though it is a stand-alone struggle. In real life, however, a person is not defined by a single area of struggle. People need discipleship, and discipleship involves spiritual nurture in all areas of life. Sexuality is one of those areas, but it is certainly not the only area for discipleship—nor is it necessarily the most important.

As significant as homosexual temptations may be in a person's life, a pastor should show concern for the whole person, not just for his or her sexual struggles. In fact, a person's struggle in sexuality is often related to other needs.

---

[71] An article in the August 1998 issue of *Newsweek* observed, "Few identities in America are more marginal than ex-gay." As marginalized as those in the homosexual community may feel, those who profess to have been changed (to be "ex-gay") are more so. (Joe Dallas, *Desires in Conflict: Hope for Men who Struggle with Sexual Identity* [Eugene, Ore.: Harvest House, 2003], 56.)

[72] See esp., Stanton L. Jones, Mark A. Yarhouse, *Ex-gays?: A Longitudinal Study of Religiously Mediated Change in Sexual Orientation* (Downers Grove, Ill.: IVP, 2007).

There may be bitterness that feeds a person's gender confusion. A person may need nurture in basic biblical disciplines in order to comprehend Scripture's instructions on sexuality.[73] Faith in the cross of Christ, with repentance for all one's sin against God, is of course foundational to any work of sanctification (including sexual renewal). Multiple discipleship issues are often intertwined in a person's life. And even where it is not possible to see connections between various areas of growth, Christ calls us to show his love to whole people in all areas of life (Matt. 28:19–20).

Rather than addressing same-sex struggles as a "special" problem, or a "condition" to be treated in isolation from all others, sexuality should be viewed as one aspect of Christian witness and discipleship.

Finally, it needs to be affirmed that the first priority in ministry to all unbelievers, whatever their particular sins and temptations, is the ministry of evangelism. Apart from the presence of God's Spirit, no victory over sin and temptation can be expected. The following guidelines are provided in that conviction.

It is God's Spirit who overcomes the sinful tendencies and resistance in our hearts. It is he who patiently softens our hearts to bring about a new longing for holiness, and who empowers us to reflect that holiness (Ezek. 36:25–27). Therefore, when ministering to those who have no evidence of the Spirit's conviction and no evidence of repentance, the first priority is the gracious call of the Gospel. God's Word calls men and women involved in sin of any kind to repent and bow the knee to Christ their Creator and the only Redeemer. The first priority in ministry to all unbelievers, whatever their particular sins and temptations, is the ministry of evangelism.

The following guidelines do not replace evangelism. Instead, they presuppose some level of responsiveness to the Spirit's work through the Gospel, bringing a desire (even if just a budding desire) for holiness in Christ.

2. Points of Guidance

The following points are intended as guidelines. They are not presented in any particular sequence, they are certainly not exhaustive, and they are not

---

[73] Cf., Chapter IV. We there showed how some Bible scholars cite Scripture in their efforts to legitimize homosexuality, but the understanding of Scripture used in those approaches is flawed. In some cases, discipleship in the nature of Scripture and the role Scripture itself calls us to give it in our lives could be important.

intended as any kind of method or outline for counseling men and women with same-sex struggles.

Because every person's situation is unique, we do not think it would be fruitful to construct a specific counseling model to follow. Instead, we have compiled various points of wisdom gleaned from our consultation with experienced counselors and their writings, from conversations with Christians who have come out of a homosexual background, and from our own ministry with men and women with same-sex temptations. We hope these guidelines will prove useful for pastors or counselors (and, in appropriate settings, laymen and congregations also) who are helping those with same-sex desires to bring their sexuality under the redemptive reign of Christ.

a. Trust—It takes a lot of courage to share personal struggles with a pastor or elder. That is true of any struggle, and it is certainly true about sexual struggles. Generally, by the time a person opens up his or her experience with same-sex temptations to a spiritual leader, there is already a long history of shame, agonizing, and guilt. It is a huge expression of trust to open up such an intimate area of need. A minister needs to understand that from the very start, and to make every effort to honor that trust, including the careful guarding of confidences and emotional sensitivity.

b. Choice—Many Christians mistakenly assume that a person is only responsible for what he has chosen. Therefore, to help an individual take responsibility for same-sex desires they feel obliged to prove that those same-sex desires were somehow cognitively chosen by the person experiencing them. This approach is inaccurate and unhelpful, both theologically and experientially. In any area of sin (not just same-sex sin), there certainly are choices involved in sinful *behaviors,* but *temptations* are not always consciously sought out. Sometimes they are; but sometimes temptation takes us by surprise. Most men and women with same-sex struggles have no awareness of ever having chosen these desires. A counselor needs to be alert to sinful choices that may be part of same-sex desires, but it is unnecessary to belabor the point or try to prove "you brought this struggle upon yourself." We are each responsible to bring our own areas of temptation and weakness to the cross, whatever their origins, and there to seek Christ's redemption and grace—including struggles we did not choose.

c. Hope and expectations—In all ministry, we must keep the full hope of glory before us with patient expectations about our experience of that glory today. God promises total redemption of our whole man, in Christ. In this life, we must continually make use of the means of grace and continually reckon ourselves dead to sin and alive to God in Christ. As we do so (through the means of grace), God's Spirit is pleased to advance our sanctification according to his wisdom. The resurrection of Christ proves to us that the victory he has won for us is real and absolute. Our experience of that victory may be quick or gradual. In one area or another, that victory may be experienced in full, or with ongoing struggle. This is true of a believer's struggles with pride, anger, gossip, lust, and other areas of temptation. Likewise, same-sex temptations must be brought continually to Christ with real hope and realistic expectations.[74]

d. Motives—A person's motives for pursuing sanctification in any area of struggle needs to be a love for Christ and his glory, not simply a desire to "fix myself" and "correct something embarrassing to me." The Spirit of Christ may work patiently or he may work quickly (see point **c**, above). Helping a person nurture godly motivations for his or her efforts in sanctification will prove fruitful. Joe Dallas, an "ex-gay" man with a prominent ministry to those with same-sex struggles, observes, "I have seen plenty of successes. But there are plenty of failures, too. And among the failures I have seen two common elements: wrong motivation and unrealistic expectations."[75] Man's chief end in every area of sanctification is the glory of God and our communion with him.

e. Identity issues—At the root of every temptation is a lie. Furthermore, God made mankind in his image, and in Christ he is renewing men and women into his image. These truths must be kept in mind when using the many labels for "homosexuality" circulating in the culture. Labels like "homosexual," "gay," "lesbian," and so forth are intended to define a person's identity. Since the believer's identity is in Christ, and we are being renewed in holiness after the likeness of Christ in every aspect of our brokenness, we must exercise

---

[74] Illustrating the variety of ways sanctification unfolds, Jones and Yarhouse summarize the testimonies of nearly 100 men and women pursuing sexual wholeness in Christ through the ministries of Exodus International. Of that group, they identify those who experienced complete transformation of their desires ("conversion"), others with some remaining struggles but significant victory ("chastity"), and others continuing to struggle but with sustained hope ("continuing"), along with some who sadly experienced no significant change and lost hope ("confused" and "gay identity"). (Stanton L. Jones and Mark A. Yarhouse, *Ex-gays*, 287–93.) These are the same kinds of experiences which might be identified in any area of temptation, not just sexual orientation struggles.

[75] Joe Dallas, *Desires in Conflict: Hope for Men who Struggle with Sexual Identity* (Eugene, Ore.: Harvest House, 2003), 44.

discernment in our use of these labels. Only God has the right to define a person; the culture (even church culture) does not have that authority. What others have said about a person's identity must be reconciled with the voice of God.

f. Wholesome fellowship—It should not be assumed that everyone with same-sex struggles grew up with poor male (for men) or female (for women) role models. Nevertheless, this is often enough the case to warrant careful attention. And even where poor relationships with same-sex role models was not present, same-sex temptations can leave a man marginalized from healthy male fellowship, and women from healthy female fellowship. An important part of ministry to men and women with sexual identity struggles is to provide wholesome, godly fellowship with others of the same gender. We're not talking about guys doing "macho" stuff to "prove" their manhood. But including a man in wholesome fellowship with other men, and a woman in godly companionship with other ladies, is tremendously important.

g. Emotional needs—God made everything and gave everything its proper purpose; Satan created nothing. Sin always involves taking something God made for good purposes and using it for wrong purposes. This is certainly true of sex and sexual desires, as well. Sometimes sexual sins—both "heterosexual" and "homosexual"—involve an effort to find emotional needs fulfilled by sex which sex was never designed to fulfill. Sometimes a person has emotional needs for belonging, for acceptance, for worth, and so on. These emotional "holes" need to be healed through the grace of Christ and godly relationships, not through ungodly imaginations or deeds. In ministry to those with same-sex temptations, a pastor or counselor should be mindful of the tendency for both "heterosexual" and "homosexual" sexualization of emotional needs.[76] The emotional needs may be legitimate, but they need to be met in proper ways.

h. Stumbling blocks—Forgiveness and redemption is the work of Christ, transforming the inner man. It is nothing we can accomplish in ourselves. Nevertheless, Christ calls us to be faithful in small things as we look to him for great things. It is a matter of such faithfulness and simply prudence to remove stumbling blocks to sin from one's life. If there are magazines, videos, internet sites, particular hang-outs or associations, or other influences that stir same-sex temptations, these should be removed as far as possible. Accountability for overcoming habits in these areas can be a valuable help.

---

[76] Joe Dallas, *Desires in Conflict*, 114–18.

i. Bitterness—God designed human sexuality to find expression between a man and a woman. By its nature, therefore, same-sex behavior is defiant (Rom. 1:26–27). This does not mean that all those who struggle with same-sex temptations are motivated by bitterness and defiance. But it does mean that bitterness can fuel same-sex desires, and same-sex desires are sometimes most deeply entrenched in the context of significant bitterness. Be ready to help a person resolve areas of bitterness and learn forgiveness.

j. Gifts and service—Do not allow discipleship to deteriorate into a consuming focus on just one issue of struggle. A person's same-sex struggles may call for prominent attention in discipleship, but encourage his or her spiritual development in other areas of life as well. This includes the development of his or her gifts for service to others. Same-sex orientation is not itself a source of giftedness. There is no biblical basis for the anecdotal claims that "same-sex orientation" enhances sensitivity or other qualities. At the same time, struggling with same-sex desires does not negate the fact that each person has gifts which need to be nurtured and brought into service of the Spirit (Rom. 12:3–8).

k. Repentance—The book of Nehemiah opens with a prayer of repentance. Nehemiah heard that the walls of Jerusalem, the city of his people and his forefathers, had been broken down. His response was to weep and repent, not only for the sins he himself had committed personally, but for the sins of his family and his nation. Such examples in Scripture are a reminder to us that sin is both individual and corporate. We all bear the curse of Adam's sin (original sin), the burden of our own family's and society's sins, along with the sins we ourselves commit. The brokenness we experience is wrapped up in the curse upon all mankind, our own societies, and ourselves, on account of the complicated mess of sin woven all throughout humankind. Repentance for each one of us involves confession of corporate sins as well as individual sins. This principle is important to remember when helping a person take responsibility for an area of brokenness like same-sex desires, which he or she may never have chosen for him/herself, but which is nonetheless a manifestation of sin to be repented of (cf., *WCF* 6.3–6).

l. Acceptance versus approval—The spirit of the Pharisees is alive and well in every age, leading us to suppose that holiness means avoiding association with people who are struggling in grievous temptations and sin. On the other hand, the spirit of Balaam is also present in every generation, urging approval of wickedness and participation in their sin. Jesus is the Good Shepherd who seeks after the wandering sheep and the Good Physician who reaches out to the spiritually sick, without however condoning sin. We should seek to represent Christ to others, including his readiness to associate with "publicans and sinners" in compassionate ministry, without approving of their sinful ways. This would include our careful readiness to show Christ's compassion to men and women caught in the web of same-sex temptations and sin (cf., Jude 23).

m. Listening—Scripture exhorts us to "be quick to hear and slow to speak" (Jas. 1:19). A quickness to listen is especially important when dealing with needs as sensitive and complex as same-sex desires. A readiness to get to know the person to whom you are ministering is important. The "quick to hear" principle also calls us to a humble willingness to read, seek counsel, and learn from others, especially when ministering in an area in which we may not have had much personal exposure before. Be a good listener as you get to know the person to whom you are ministering. And for further resources on ministry to those with same-sex struggles, see the resource list on pp. 66–67, below.

n. Prayer — Prayer is essential. In prayer, we acknowledge our dependence on the Spirit's intervention to accomplish our sanctification. In prayer, we rest our hope upon the Spirit for his mighty blessing on our otherwise fruitless efforts. Pray for those to whom you are ministering. Pray with them, too. Praying with them helps to strengthen their awareness of God's reality and presence with them in their struggles. Remember that the Father delights to answer prayer.

These fourteen points of guidance are not exhaustive. And most of these points are standard principles for counseling relevant for ministry to any area of struggle. But we have endeavored to show the application of various discipleship principles to same-sex temptations, specifically.

For further perspective on the history and theology of sexual orientation issues, and on ministry to those struggling with same-sex desires, an annotated list of reference materials follows.

3. Select, Annotated Bibliography

The following list is deliberately abbreviated. A full bibliography of texts can be derived from the many footnotes throughout this paper, and through the bibliographies of those works. We have identified, below, a few titles which we believe to be among the most helpful to recommend for pastors and other Christian leaders desiring to read further.

a. Theological and Apologetic Resources—accessible

Dan O. Via and Robert A. J. Gagnon, *Homosexuality and the Bible: Two Views* (Minneapolis: Fortress Press, 2003), 117 pages with bibliography and Scripture index—This book is a short but robust presentation of two leading representatives of opposite positions on Scripture and homosexuality. In a typical "two views" format, each author presents his own position at length, and the book closes with short rebuttals from each responding to the other's material.

Greg L. Bahnsen, *Homosexuality: A Biblical View* (Grand Rapids: Baker, 1978), 152 pages—although over 30 years old, Bahnsen's perceptive treatment of the subject is still worthy of note. Bahnsen's book addresses the subject from a reformed perspective, with awareness of the scientific issues already emerging in his day.

R. Albert Mohler, Jr., *Desire and Deceit: The Real Cost of the New Sexual Tolerance* (Colorado Springs: Multnomah, 2008), 160 pages—an almost pocket-sized book, this book is a succinct review of the history and theology behind the homosexual movement, with insightful observations regarding the implications of mainstreaming homosexuality upon society.

b. Theological and Apologetic Resources—scholarly

Robert A. J. Gagnon, *The Bible and Homosexual Practice: Texts and Hermeneutics* (Nashville: Abingdon, 2001), 520 pages with author, Scripture, and classical texts indexes—one of the most extensive, exegetical and theological treatments on homosexuality and Scripture to date. Gagnon's conclusions on the subject are in line with the positions espoused in the present paper.

Stanton L. Jones, Mark A. Yarhouse, *Ex-gays?: A Longitudinal Study of Religiously Mediated Change in Sexual Orientation* (Downers Grove, Ill.: IVP, 2007), 414 pages with subject index—written by psychologists for psychologists using standard research methods of modern psychology, this book presents the leading scientific case that religious approaches have demonstrated effectiveness in bringing about change to homosexual orientation.

c. Pastoral Resources

Joe Dallas, *Desires in Conflict: Hope for Men Who Struggle with Sexual Identity* (Eugene, Ore.: Harvest House, 2003), 247 pages with suggested reading list by subject—written by a man who came to Christ and found deliverance from a gay lifestyle. Joe Dallas now speaks, writes, and counsels to help others find salvation and sexual wholeness in Christ. This book is a hopeful yet realistic, practical, and helpful guide for men dealing with same-sex struggles. It is addressed directly to men struggling with same-sex desires, making it a useful resource for reading with someone in a discipleship setting.

Anne Paulk, *Restoring Sexual Identity: Hope for Women Who Struggle with Same-Sex Attraction* (Eugene, Ore.: Harvest House, 2003), 272 pages with suggested reading list by subject—written by a woman who came to Christ and found deliverance from a lesbian lifestyle, this volume is the counterpart to Joe Dallas's book for men above. In this book, Anne Paulk addresses herself to women wrestling with same-sex desires, making this a useful resource for two women to read together in a discipleship setting.

Exodus International Ministries
(website: http://www.exodusinternational.org/). Exodus International is on the forefront of ministry to men and women with same-sex struggles. There are numerous resources available on their website, as well as conferences and regional contacts they provide for support.